Event Management for the Tourism and Hospitality Industries

Event Management for the Tourism and Hospitality Industries provides a theoretical and practical approach to teach students of Tourism and Hospitality the basics of planning, managing and evaluating all types of events.

Chapters cover skills such as visitor segmentation, product analysis, developing a budget, promotion and after-event assessment. Special emphasis is placed on critical issues now facing event managers, such as environmental sustainability and awareness of cultural diversity, technology and community engagement. The reader will learn the necessity of connecting events with community heritage and culture to provide the local, personalized experienced desired by visitors. Each chapter covers a unique step in the planning process and corresponds to a section of a detailed event plan outline found at the end of the book that can be submitted as a semester-long assignment. Making use of international case studies in every chapter, this book provides real-world examples to contextualize the information given.

This will be essential reading for all Tourism and Hospitality students with an interest in Events Management and Design, and for practitioners employed in tour companies, cruise ships, destination management organizations and cultural festivals.

Bonita M. Kolb, PhD is Professor Emeritus at Lycoming College in the United States. She currently resides in St. Augustine, Florida, where she is actively working with companies in the hospitality industries.

Event Management for the Tourism and Hospitality Industries

Bonita M. Kolb

Routledge
Taylor & Francis Group

LONDON AND NEW YORK

First published 2022
by Routledge
2 Park Square, Milton Park, Abingdon, Oxon OX14 4RN

and by Routledge
605 Third Avenue, New York, NY 10158

Routledge is an imprint of the Taylor & Francis Group, an informa business

British Library Cataloguing-in-Publication Data
A catalogue record for this book is available from the British Library

Library of Congress Cataloging-in-Publication Data
Names: Kolb, Bonita M, author.
Title: Event management for the tourism and
hospitality industries / Bonita M Kolb.
Description: Abingdon, Oxon; New York, NY: Routledge, 2021. |
Includes bibliographical references and index.
Identifiers: LCCN 2021004775 (print) | LCCN 2021004776 (ebook)
Subjects: LCSH: Special events–Management. | Tourism–Management.
| Tourism–Planning. | Hospitality industry–Management. |
Hospitality industry–Planning.
Classification: LCC GT3405 .K56 2021 (print) | LCC GT3405 (ebook) |
DDC 394.2068–dc23
LC record available at https://lccn.loc.gov/2021004775
LC ebook record available at https://lccn.loc.gov/2021004776

ISBN: 9780367649975 (hbk)
ISBN: 9780367649920 (pbk)
ISBN: 9781003127321 (ebk)

Typeset in Frutiger and Sabon
by Deanta Global Publishing Services, Chennai, India

Contents

Cases

Chapter 1

Meeting changing event visitor expectations

Abstract

Events can provide a source of visitors for both the tourism and hospitality industries. Rather than only relying on existing events and attractions, tourism and hospitality managers can work together to create new events to attract visitors. There are many types of events that can be created but all are intangible service products, which makes them difficult to promote. Visitors have the opportunity of many competing events to attend. They want events that provide an authentic experience that is representative of the local community. To choose the right event the organization needs to analyze the community to determine what type of experience it can offer. Visitors are savvy consumers who conduct social media research to learn about the experience of previous visitors. The event chosen to attend becomes part of the visitor's sense of self-identity. There are many different types of events including sports, entertainment, heritage and culture. Events can also be packaged around visitors' interest in the environment or volunteering. The event should have the support of the community and lead to economic development.

Creating visitor events

Hospitality and tourism, along with companies managing events, can all be categorized as service providers. Beyond providing for basic needs such as food and shelter these industries provide an experience that appeals to the emotions of visitors. The hospitality industry consists of lodging and food establishments. It has traditionally been defined as providing the basic human needs of shelter and food for people who are traveling. As the industry matured and became more competitive it was necessary for hotels and restaurants to distinguish themselves based on the type of experience they provided. It was no longer enough to only provide food and shelter. They needed to provide an experience that added to the enjoyment of the overall visit. The tourism industry has also needed to adapt as visitors' expectations have changed. Visitors who were once happy simply to be able to take a holiday have become increasingly demanding as to the type and quality of experience they desire (Abel 2020). They want authenticity but also an enjoyable experience.

Both the hospitality and tourism industries have realized that a reliable source of visitors has been events (Van Eck 2018). Business meetings, conferences and exhibitions have been a major source of visitors for destinations. These events might be sponsored by individual companies, nonprofit organizations or associations that represent industry sectors. The visitors to these events would need both food and lodging which provided revenue to the hospitality sector. While the primary purpose of attendance was not to be a tourist, those attending often wanted to visit local sites and attractions which provided revenue to the tourism industry.

Major events such as music concerts and sporting competitions served the same purpose of providing revenue to both the hospitality and tourism industries. For this reason, both the hospitality and tourism industries actively promoted events to attract these types of events to their communities. Now, rather than only trying to attract existing events, hospitality and tourism are being proactive in creating and promoting their own events in their communities.

Industry distinctions

- Hospitality: Provides lodging and food.
- Tourism: Attracts visitors to area attractions.
- Event management: Plans and implements activities.

Connections between hospitality, tourism and event industries

The field of hospitality management can be defined as applying management concepts to the areas of lodging, dining and general guest services. The hospitality industry provides food and lodging to tourists but also to business travelers, and people simply traveling through the area. Tourism management studies is a broad term that applies to attracting tourists to an area by providing places and activities of interest. Tourism managers try to attract events to their city or promote existing events as it provides economic benefit to the hotels, restaurants and general economy. Event management applies management concepts to the planning and running of all types of events. All three of these industries will be needed to attract additional visitors to a community. One way to do so is to create new events rather than only attract visitors to the existing ones. Hospitality managers, tourism organizations and event planners will all be involved in creating these new events that will bring visitors and revenue to the community.

Professional event planners are used because of the complexity of large events and the increasing demands by attendees. Event planners must organize the various essential components such as food, lodging and transportation. Added to this are the elements that make each event unique and personalized to the desires of the attendees. It is not surprising that event managers are critical participants in organizing large-scale civic, government and community events.

Hospitality management has largely focused on the experience of the guest while at the hotel. Some personal events such as weddings might be held at a hotel and the catering department would assist in the planning while also encouraging the booking of rooms. Business events held at hotels would involve the hospitality manager in the planning of the needed logistics of meeting rooms and technology. These events were also a driver of room bookings. What has changed is that the hospitality industry has started to plan and promote its own events (Shankman 2019). The experience of staying at the hotel is now considered not just a logistical necessity but can be incorporated and themed into an event.

The tourism and hospitality industries are unique, as they are a combination of government-funded organizations, nonprofits and private businesses. Tourism promotion agencies such as destination marketing organizations and visitor bureaus that provide information are often funded by the government. Some tourism attractions such as museums and historical sites may be governed by boards of nonprofits. Finally, there will be private businesses such as restaurants, hotels and attractions. The size of any of these organizations can range from large, such as Disneyworld, to a local farmers' market run by volunteers.

Tourism professionals have always marketed their communities as places to visit. Now the task is more complicated as visitors want a complete experience not just an opportunity to get away from home. Events that can meet this need may already exist, in which case the tourism department only needs to develop promotional messages. If events do not exist that will attract visitors it will be necessary to work with the community to develop them. As a result of this need to create events, hospitality managers and tourism professionals now need the skills involved in professional event management.

Purpose of events

Events is a broad term that includes how people can come together for education, enjoyment, celebration or all three. Events can first be divided into those that are personal, locally attended and those that are planned to attract visitors to the area. Personal events are held to mark the milestones of life. Some come yearly such as birthdays and anniversaries. Less frequently held and therefore more elaborate are events to mark births, weddings and funerals. For most people, these types of events have been planned by family members. Now professional event managers are hired to help with planning and then managing the event. Industries hold private events for both the purpose of educating industry members and providing socialization opportunities. These events were restricted to industry members and their guests. Professional event planners are needed to plan and implement the event. They would work with tourism and hospitality professionals to provide lodging and additional experiences.

Local events were held by the community to commemorate historic anniversaries, celebrate local culture or have a sporting competition. These events might be organized by a religious organization, a private civic club or by a government agency. The holding of the event was an occasion for a leisure activity to break up the routine tasks of life. Such civic events allowed members of the community to socialize while they also reinforced shared personal and cultural values. Because these events were only for the local community, tourism and hospitality industries were not involved.

There is now a growing interest by visitors in participating in these types of events. As the world becomes more global there is desire to maintain a link with authentic local culture. Tourism and hospitality can take advantage of this interest by promoting these events to visitors. If there are no such events, they can work with the community to create an event.

Purpose of event

- Celebration: Honor an event, group or person.
- Education: Personal development.
- Enjoyment: Fun and socialization.
- Economic development: Help local businesses.

Events as a service product

In the past, events were less complex to plan and implement, as simply having a chance for leisure and an opportunity to meet people not ordinarily encountered may have been enough to motivate attendance. People's expectations are now much higher. To meet these expectations, events have become a product that is conceived, designed, packaged and sold, the same as any product. All events, from a small local festival to a major sporting event, are service products that have several elements that make them uniquely different from a tangible product, such as shoes or furniture, that is sold to consumers.

Service products are differentiated from tangible products by such characteristics as being intangible, inseparable and perishable. While there might be tangible, or physical, elements to an event, such as gifts given to attendees at weddings, welcome bags left in hotel rooms or souvenirs for purchase at tourism locations, these alone are not the motivation for attendance. The motivation is the intangible experience of being at the event. This presents a challenge when promoting the event. While it is easy to use a photo of shoes or furniture when promoting a tangible product, it is more difficult to promote the intangible experience of attendance at an event that has not yet happened.

Events are also inseparable. This term refers to the fact that the product can only happen at a specific time and place. The place would not only include the physical venue and the geographic location, but also includes the ambience, style and atmosphere created using the physical space. In addition, the people encountered at the event are often as important as the event itself. "Who else will be there?" is not a casual question but instead is integral to the decision of whether to attend. Finally, the staff at the event are not just there to serve, they are also a part of the event experience. Their appearance and attitude either add to the success of the event or detract from it.

The characteristic of a service product being perishable will affect the attendance and revenue of an event. Perishability refers to the fact that by their nature events are limited to a specific time period. If a person chooses not to attend, that visitor and the revenue that would have been gained has been lost forever. If the event is not well attended it cannot be extended or held the next week. This is why promotion to ensure attendance and the success of the event is crucial. While an unsold physical product does not disappear and therefore can be sold the next day, once an event is past, it is too late to attract attendance.

Visitor motivation

The expectations of travelers have changed. In the early days of hospitality and tourism, simply having a destination that met basic needs was enough. A safe place to sleep, good food and something interesting to see was all that was expected. Now the visitor wants a unique experience that they can not only enjoy but can then share online with others. This sharing is not just for enjoyment but is also a means of bragging. Half of young travelers state that when making a travel decision, how it will be perceived on their social media sites is a consideration (Taylor 2019).

It will take tourism, hospitality and event management professionals working together to create these types of events. Together they have the ability to create the locally authentic experience that visitors now seek. The only way to experience the event is to be physically present. People who visit the community then help the community by boosting the local economy. A further benefit to communities that create such events is that they are harder for competing cities to replicate. While many communities can promote a sports stadium, art museum or theme parks, an event based on the unique character of a community can't be easily replicated. In addition, staging an event unique to a community, while involving expense, is still much less costly than building a new tourism attraction. Finally, because so many cities are now intercultural, events have become an effective way of sharing culture with visitors while building community at home.

Advantages of creating local events

- Grows local economy.
- Difficult for other communities to replicate.
- Less costly than building attractions.
- Builds community.

Attendance motivation

The motivation for attending an event may simply be social, such as the need to interact with community members. Small-scale events such as farmer's markets and Saturday night movies in a public park can meet this need. Attending a larger event that attracts visitors from outside the area provides an opportunity to meet people that would ordinarily not be encountered. The motivation to attend an event might be the need for relaxation when daily life becomes too stressful. The opposite is also true. People might attend events because they are bored with their day-to-day routine and want stimulation. In both cases, attending an event either close to home or at a distance can mean that they return home refreshed. The expectations of consumers are always changing (Mimaroglu 2019). Social media provides the ability to monitor these changing expectations as they happen.

Event tourism

Because of rising incomes people have the ability to travel to events instead of only attending those close to home. Traveling to events might have been an occasional treat but has now become commonplace. When traveling to events, visitors want more than just socialization and relaxation. They now want to not only have fun but also learn while having new experiences.

In the past it was thought that only a few visitors were interested in a learning experience (Stavans 2015). People with the money to travel also had the education to appreciate the cultural heritage of the destination they were visiting. In contrast, it was thought that most tourists were lacking in time, money and education. As a result, they wanted to book inexpensive preplanned trips that only provided enjoyment. They did not wish to learn anything new about their destination but wanted experiences that conformed to their existing preconceptions of the place.

One of the early models to capture the varying and often simultaneous motivations for traveling to events is still relevant when discussing visitor motivation. Visitors have been traditionally divided into people motivated by a desire for escapism and those who are motivated by a desire to seek experiences (Iso-Ahola 1980). Although the motivations may overlap, the two groups differ in what they seek. Escape travelers want fewer stimuli from their travel, not more. The visitor motivated by a desire to escape doesn't want to take a trip that is challenging, as they want to get away from stress and simply enjoy themselves. On the other hand, experience visitors seek new stimuli. They travel because of a desire to experience a new culture or engage in an activity. As a result, they want new and unique experiences that they will document and then share.

A more recent model for visitor motivation focuses on how they wish to interact with the community they visit (Gilmore and Pine 2007). Groups of visitors can be categorized as followers, explorers or adventurers based on the level of interaction they prefer. Followers have read about a place that is popular and then visit so they can check it off their list. Once at the destination they are less interested in exploring and only wish to view the major sites. Visitors can also be categorized as explorers. They will also visit well-known places, but they will also want to explore the community. They are not truly adventurous, as they will only be interested in exploring what others have experienced. Adventurer visitors have always wanted to experience the real community. They want to discover and experience something beyond what is directly connected with the event.

Social media has impacted all three types of visitors (Bosangit 2014). In the past, visitors were often on their own in finding sites and experiences. Now this information is shared through blogs, video and photo-sharing sites. Followers use social media review sites to find the most popular places to visit. Explorers will use these sites to find events that fit their individual interests while providing them with the opportunity to interact with local community members, as they desire an authentic, personalized experience. Adventurers will visit places that are not yet on social media. They will then document through blogs and videos their experiences and then share them online. This sharing is a critical component of the visitor experience, not an afterthought. Social media sharing of unique experiences has resulted in an increased desire for evermore authentic, unique and personalized travel experiences among explorers and even followers.

Visitor expectations

The easy access to information on social media has changed consumers' expectations of how products should be marketed. They now demand that any travel experience they purchase be represented accurately. The choice of destination is felt to be a reflection on the visitor's self-image. Travel is used not just for enjoyment but also to enhance and share online their sense of identity. Attending an event that is not as it was promoted is not only making a purchasing mistake; it affects the visitor's sense of who they are.

To get accurate information, potential visitors rely on the advice of those who have already visited. In fact, sharing information on travel has become part of the travel experience. That this behavior starts even before the trip can be seen by the fact that 50 percent of travelers download phone apps for the location they will be visiting when researching a potential travel destination (Manoukian 2019). Because they know so much about a destination before visiting, visitors are no longer satisfied with the standard tourist experience; instead they want a unique experience that is personalized to their interests and reflects their identity. The challenge for tourism and hospitality organizations is learning more about visitor desires so that this type of personalized event can be provided.

Desire for authentic and personalized experiences

Another issue that relates to the current change in tourism consumer behavior is the type of experience desired. Earlier studies of tourism were built on the idea that tourists wanted to have an experience different than daily life. Travel was seen as an escape from reality. Now what travelers want is to be part of an authentic local experience that fits their individual interests.

Authenticity can have a variety of meanings, depending on the context in which the word is used (Knudsen and Waade 2010). Applying the term to destinations means that their reality is both credibly and reliably represented. Any Disneyland theme park is authentically Disney in that it provides the experience that the tourist expects when visiting. Authenticity can also mean that something exists and is not imaginary. While people can view videos about a country and a culture online, this is not considered to be an authentic experience, as would visiting personally be. Lastly, authenticity can mean that a place is the original and not a copy. The intensity of an experience is increased and an emotional relationship is created when encountering an original place or culture. The most authentic tourism experiences can be said to be a credible encounter with the original place that generates a feeling of relationship. The search for authenticity by visitors can be defined as a desire to experience life as it is really lived somewhere else.

Even if in the past travelers wanted a unique travel experience, they lacked both the knowledge of the destination and the ability to access tourism providers directly. As a result, they needed to rely on travel intermediaries to book their trip. To please the most travelers, these intermediaries tended to standardize the travel experience by providing similar experiences. Now people are no longer satisfied with this standardized approach to tourism. Because they are globally aware through reading about and viewing destinations online, they want to do more than simply see a place. Instead they want to experience the local culture in a way that technology can't provide. While they are looking for cultural difference, they want experiences that mirror their already existing interests and lifestyles. For example, if visitors are interested in music, photography or sports at home, they will want to experience the local cultural expression of the same. Tourism and hospitality managers will need to conduct research to determine what type of authentic experience is desired so that it can be provided by a community-based event.

Community analysis for event potential

One of the first steps in the process of developing a marketing plan to attract tourists to events is to determine what the city or town has to offer potential visitors. Analyzing the city as a product can be difficult because the local residents may no longer notice the city's history, beauty, educational institutions, cultural opportunities or even climate, as they are taken for granted.

When analyzing the city as a site for events the focus should not only be on the city's features and services but also on the benefits the experience of visiting can provide.

These benefits will be promoted with a message that connects emotionally. Because potential visitors have many destination options, they will not take the risk to visit somewhere new unless assured of the benefits they will receive.

For example, visiting historic sites related to the founding of the country can provide visitors with the benefit of reinforcing their national values or pride. Visiting a city might also allow visitors to enjoy entertainment options that provide the benefit of excitement that is not found in their everyday lives. Visitors may also visit an event that includes a cultural performance to receive the benefit of a quality arts experience that is not available to them at home. A visit to an amusement park can provide the benefit of time for family togetherness. Visiting an exhibit by a contemporary artist can reinforce an identity as a trendsetter if this same artist cannot be seen at home. Finally, a cooking lesson can develop a new skill that can be used after they return home. The analysis of the city as a product to discover both the features and the benefits it provides is one of the most important steps in the development of a new event.

Often overlooked as a benefit is the attractiveness of the infrastructure of the city, which will need to be analyzed for its potential to appeal to visitors. This includes the cleanliness and attractiveness of the streets and sidewalks and also the condition of the buildings and their architectural style. Other physical features that should be noted when analyzing the community are the condition of the city's streets along with the amenities provided such as benches, landscaping, lighting and signage. In addition the availability of any parks, bike paths, waterways, rivers or canals should be noted. These features will need to be analyzed as to whether they are attractive or need to be improved.

The city's critical first impression to a visitor can be described as the packaging that envelops the event just as a box surrounds a purchased product. While difficult to analyze, it is a critical component of the event's image that will be promoted. This first impression includes the community's character, image, accessibility and human interaction. For example, upon arrival to attend a music festival or an event at a transportation museum, the visitor will first notice the overall cleanliness of the city. They will also notice the style of the buildings, the availability of parking and if the local residents are helpful in providing them with any needed information. It doesn't take a physical visit to the city to make this assessment. Potential visitors will use the websites sponsored by tourism and lodging organizations. They will use photo-sharing sites to see photos posted by other visitors. If the potential visitor's first impression is negative, they will not be interested in attending the event.

Analyzing community infrastructure

- Streets and sidewalks: Cleanliness, directional signage, seating.
- Buildings: Clearly addressed, historical plaques, landscaping.
- Stores: Open hours posted, attractive window displays, storefronts maintained.
- Public areas: Flowers or planters, public art, cleanliness, trash receptacles.
- Safety: Adequate lighting, signage for assistance.

Creating an event with community support

There are a number of different segments of tourists that can be targeted based on the type of event. Tourism and hospitality organizations should consider several ideas before moving forward in development. Sporting event tourism, cultural tourism, heritage tourism and eco-tourism each can be attractive to distinct visitor groups.

Types of events

- Sports: Participation or viewing.
- Cultural: Exploration of customs.
- Heritage: Honoring the past.
- Environmental and volunteer: Improving the community.

Sport event tourism

Fans of particular teams can build a lifestyle around their support. Because of their willingness to spend money on tickets and travel, cities have been willing to invest in expensive stadiums to attract fans. Additional events can be easily developed around existing game schedules. Adding elements such as meet and greets, tours of practice facilities and an opportunity to walk on the field will all be additional motives to travel to an event. Once at the event, the sports fan and family members will then be interested in adding on other tourism activities that are not part of the event, bringing in even more revenue.

This model works well for major cities that are home to well-known teams. It can also work for smaller communities who have sports that have loyal, but smaller fan bases. These sports are often part of the heritage of the region. Nine-pin bowling, ping-pong, curling and bocce ball are sports that people don't just watch, they also play. If a community is known for a local sport, an event can be created where fans get to meet each other while participating in amateur competitions.

Cultural event tourism

People have always traveled to experience arts, including visual, music and performance. The tourism and hospitality organizations in an area can use a new cultural venue, performance or exhibit as the core of an event. All that is needed is the creativity to see the potential. For example, an exhibit by a well-known French painter can also include a showing of French films. A food festival can be held that demonstrates how to easily cook French food at home. Allowing fans to paint their own French masterpieces can be a fun family activity. Even a vendor selling French perfumes would be a possible attraction that could be added. Dedicated cultural tourists were already going to attend. The event is to attract the visitor who needs the added motivation of additional benefits.

The same approach can be developed by smaller communities, who may be in the town where a famous artist or musician was born. There might be a local art form such as using botanicals to die fabric that can be the core of an event. Along with the opportunity to watch artists at work, there would be the opportunity for visitors to create objects that they could then take home as a souvenir. These types of events can be targeted to families as having both cultural and educational benefits.

Heritage event tourism

Heritage events can be built on the traditions of local residents. These can attract visitors that wish to share that heritage or visitors who are merely curious. The connection can be in the past. For example, a small town in the US state of Florida, the flattest state in the country, is called Switzerland because it was the home country of the original European settler. While the connection is now gone, an event exploring that heritage can still be created. This is where thinking of an event from the point of view of as many of the five senses as possible can be useful. If the connection is to a local heritage, there should be food to taste, art to see, music to listen to and crafts to create with their own hands.

Environmental and volunteer event tourism

People are aware that tourism and large-scale events can cause harm to a community. Many travelers research whether tourism attractions and lodging establishments are looking to minimize this impact. Visitors might also make the decision to avoid destinations that are over-visited. There is now an opportunity to build an event where these concerned visitors can help, rather than harm, a community. Such events involve volunteering to improve the community by taking action. This might be a cleanup of a local stream to improve water quality or improving hiking trails to minimize erosion.

The people who are willing to travel to a destination to be involved in such an effort will still need a place to stay and will still want to be entertained. The events that are planned must be low impact to the environment but still provide entertaining benefits to the visitor.

Community support

It is tempting, once the decision to launch an event is made, to start developing agendas, assigning tasks and getting to work. The step before doing so is to take time to decide exactly why the event is being held. The reason for having the event should be more than just to attract visitors. Such a broad mission does not provide any direction when difficult decisions on the type of event, who will be targeted and the price that will be charged need to be made.

There are more reasons for an event than attracting paying visitors. For example, the event might also involve providing employment to local businesses. It might provide opportunity for local entrepreneurs to develop new services. A component of the event could be to attract visitors who might wish to relocate to the community. The event could be held to attract the attention of large employers that the community would be an attractive place for their employees to live if the business is considering relocating. All of these can be reasons that the community will support the event.

Economic development

Everyone understands that tourists coming to a community for an event will spend money. They will need to purchase food, lodging and also spend money on transportation, even if it is only fuel for their own vehicle. Other optional visitor purchases are tickets to attractions and tours and also the purchase of souvenirs. In addition, the visitor will make purchases not directly related to the travel experience. They may buy other local products such as food at markets. In addition, they may need to purchase the necessities of life at local drug stores. They may even need additional clothing when the weather changes unexpectedly.

Even businesses that never sell directly to visitors can benefit economically from tourism. "The multiplier effect" is an economics term that refers to the fact that owners and employees of businesses that do not sell directly to visitors will also benefit indirectly. For example, if the local tour bus operator sells more tickets, the owner's income will increase. They then will be able to raise the wages paid to their employees and also have additional income for themselves. They and their employees will then be able to spend more money in the community. This additional money can show up as more revenue at the local pub or in a purchase at a local furniture store.

The more tourism services that are provided to visitors by small businesses or creative entrepreneurs within the community, the larger the multiplier effect will be, as the money spent at local businesses will stay in the community and be multiplied. Tourism services that are provided by companies that are located outside the community may be necessary, which will result in less of the money made from tourists staying in the community to be re-spent at local businesses.

Discussion questions

1. Why do professionals in tourism and hospitality need to work together when creating new events that provide a complete package of experiences for the visitor?
2. Why are service products such as events difficult to promote?
3. How have the benefits desired from attending events evolved due to technology and social changes?
4. Why does an event need to be perceived as authentic?
5. Why is the first step in creating an event a community analysis?
6. What different types of events can be created?
7. Why is community support critical to event success?

Case

Don't wait to partner with a festival – start your own!

Multiday music festivals are usually associated with camping out, which meant sleeping on the ground and using communal toilets. In exchange the music fan received days of uninterrupted music and the chance to indulge in activities not approved of at home. This might have been alright for music lovers when they were young but now that they are older and have money, they want the excitement without the discomfort. The W Hotel in Barcelona knew that visitors who stayed at their hotels tended to work hard and also party hard. They decided they could attract these visitors to stay more often and spend more money by temporarily turning their hotels into music festivals. How?

• The rooms were blocked for festival attenders, a stage was built over the pool and meeting rooms became party rooms.

- Guests were attracted because they could enjoy the music with smaller crowds and the opportunity to mingle with the artists at the bar.
- The mood was set early with wristband booths in the lobby.
- In each room was a party gift pack with breath mints – for those who wanted to get close – and condoms – for those who wanted to get even closer!

This event was initiated by the W Hotel in Barcelona who gave no thought to the guests leaving the hotel, but they could have partnered with the local tourism organization to provide additional events in the community thereby sharing the wealth (Marikar 2018).

Task: Choose a genre of music for a hotel festival. What kind of events could be packaged with the event to get people into the community?

Case

Hotels partner with the community to provide a local experience

Events designed for business people were held at hotels to provide networking opportunities. Meetings, dinners and networking were held as much as possible at the same hotel so people could interact. This was thought to be for the convenience of the business person, as it was thought that they were only interested in work. Now tourism organizations understand that business travelers don't want a homogenized experience where all they encounter is other business people. They want a sense of place that comes with connecting the past and current culture of the community.

Local hotels and tourism organizations can be involved in this process of creating tours and events for business people. To ensure success, the visitors signing up for the business conference can be surveyed as to what would be of interest. However the Hoxton Hotels in Europe and the US go further by ensuring that interacting with the community is part of the hotel experience for business visitors.

- Local businesses are offered the chance to use their meeting rooms providing visiting business people staying at the hotel a chance to interact with locals.
- Before a Hoxton Hotel opens, people from the community are asked to choose their favorite books that are then left in the hotel rooms.
- The community residents are also asked to put on bookmarks their favorite local experiences.

- To make sure the connection with the community is continued after opening, each Hoxton Hotel has a cultural marketing manager that organizes talks, film screenings and local art exhibits to which both hotel guests and area residents are invited.

Who knows what business connections, and friendships, might result (Palmer 2019)?

Task: Choose a type of local cultural experience. How can hotels and tourism organizations work together to provide events in hotels based on this authentic experience?

Event plan: Use the information from this chapter to complete the first section of the event plan outline at the end of the book.

References

Abel, Anna. 2020. "Travel Trends in 2020: Privacy, Sustainability, and More in Luxury." *Forbes.* January 8, 2020. https://www.forbes.com/sites/annabel/2020/01/08/2020s-t ravel-privacy-sustainability-and-6-more-trends-to-know/#71938b273d56. Accessed September 4, 2020.

Bosangit, C. 2014. "Online Blogs as a Marketing Tool." In *The Routledge Handbook of Tourism Marketing.* Scott McCabe (ed.) London: Routledge, 268–280.

Gilmore, J.H., and B.J. Pine. 2007. *Authenticity: What Consumers Really Want.* Boston, MA: Harvard Business School Press.

Iso-Ahola, S.E. 1980. *The Social Psychology of Leisure and Tourism.* Ann Arbor: W.C. Brown Company Publishers. University of Michigan.

Knudsen, B., and A. Waade. 2010. "Performative Authenticity in Tourism and Spatial Experience: Rethinking the Relations between Travel, Place and Emotion." In *Re-investing Authenticity: Tourism, Place and Emotions.* Britta Timm Knudsen and Anne Marit Waade (eds.) Bristol: Channel View Publications, 1–19.

Manoukian, Julia. 2019. "The Ultimate List of Travel Statistics for 2019 & 2020." *CrowdRiff.* September 23, 2019. https://crowdriff.com/resources/blog/travel-statistics. Accessed December 9, 2020.

Marikar, Sheila. 2018. "Wristbands and Room Service: Music Festivals Check into Hotels." *New York Times.* December 27, 2018. https://www.nytimes.com/2018/12/27/travel/hot els-music-festivals.html. Accessed August 10, 2020.

Mimaroglu, Alp. 2019. "How to Keep Up with Customer Expectations." *Entrepreneur.* September 30, 2019. https://www.entrepreneur.com/article/336926. Accessed August 14, 2020.

Palmer, Barbara. 2019. "Bringing a 'Sense of Place' to Meeting Design." *PCMA.* February 1, 2019. https://www.pcma.org/sense-place-travel-trend-changing-event-design/. Accessed July 14, 2020.

Shankman, Samantha. 2019. "Boutique Hotel Brands Rethink Grand Opening Events to Loop in Community." *Skift*. September 10, 2019. https://skift.com/2019/09/10/boutique -hotel-brands-rethink-grand-opening-events-to-loop-in-community/. Accessed November 11, 2020.

Stavans, I., and J. Ellison. 2015. *Reclaiming Travel*. Durham, NC: Duke University Press.

Taylor, Mia. 2019. "The Travel Motivations of Americans in 2019." *Travel Pulse*. February 2, 2019. https://www.travelpulse.com/news/features/the-travel-motivations-of-americans -in-2019.html. Accessed July 27, 2020.

Van Eck, Glenn. 2018. "The Role of Events on Tourism." *BizCommunity*. December 5, 2018. https://www.bizcommunity.com/Article/1/595/185051.html. Accessed November 5, 2020.

Chapter 2

Assessing the community for event potential

Abstract

Planning is essential for the success of any event. A business plan will describe the targeted visitor group, the type of event and the sources of revenue. A marketing plan includes the event message and how it will be communicated. A strategic plan combines these elements along with an analysis of the internal and external environments. An event will need adequate resources including financial and staffing. Both the physical environment and the people in a community must be analyzed to determine event potential. The choice of event will depend on what the community has to offer. It may involve cultural, entertainment or sporting events. There may be tours and souvenirs themed to the event. The availability of supporting products will need to be assessed. Food establishments that fit the preferences of the targeted visitor segment need to listed. Lodging by type and theme should be analyzed. Transportation availability needs to be assessed for adequacy.

Necessity of planning

Before the serious planning for the event begins, there is a need to understand what type of planning will be needed. Often mentioned are business plans and marketing plans with each serving a specific purpose. A business plan explains how the organization will operate on a daily basis while a marketing plan focuses on the promotion of the product. Both types of information are included in strategic plans. While developing a strategic plan for an event takes time, doing so will help ensure the success of the event.

It is useful to consider how this type of planning is used by potential visitors. If an expensive holiday is being planned, it makes sense for the traveler to first determine the objective for the trip. They may be taking a holiday as a way for the family to bond, to get away from a stressful job or to learn a new language. The traveler cannot plan the trip details unless they first understand the purpose of the trip. They will also need to have a budget for their trip, which is an important component of any plan. There is no reason to plan a trip that they cannot afford to take. They will then need to sell the idea for the planned to trip to who else will be traveling, which is part of a marketing plan. The strategic part of the planning would be deciding what places will be visited on what dates. Putting all this information together would ensure that the trip will succeed.

Event planning also should not begin before these types of issues have been analyzed. The resulting strategic plan will provide the event with the best chance of success. The strategic plan will start by describing the mission and vision of the organization sponsoring the event. The plan will then explain the type of event and the objective of the event, or why it is being held. The process of strategic planning will then look internally at the organization to determine what strengths can be used, such as strong marketing skills, a vibrant community or the availability of funds. Organizational weaknesses will also be analyzed so that they can be corrected. Weaknesses might include a lack of adequate staff or not having community partnerships.

The organization will then look externally. Rather than just choose an idea for an event on what the organization would like to do, it is critical to look at what type of event would be most attractive to visitors. This would depend on such external factors as the current state of the economy and current trends in tourism and hospitality. An expensive event when the economy is poor or an event based on a travel trend no longer of interest to the public will be unsuccessful no matter how meticulously it is planned.

Business and marketing plan elements

Once the strategic vision for the event is known, the focus of planning changes to who might be attracted to the event. Not all visitor segments will be attracted to a specific event. To learn more about who can be targeted as a potential visitor, the plan will detail any research that will need to be conducted.

To again use the example of planning a personal holiday, the strategic plan would include all the details of the trip: wWhere they will stay, what they will do and how they will get there. It will also include a detailed budget of what can be spent for each item on their agenda. Likewise, the strategic plan for an event will include a budget for each event item. It will also include what visitors will be charged for any additional activities.

Finally, the person planning the holiday might develop a marketing message to sell their ideas to the other people going on the trip. The marketing plan for an event would include a message on how visitors will benefit from attendance. It would then explain how the message will be communicated using traditional media or via social media.

Event strategic plans

The strategic plan both describes the event and explains its viability. There are features of a strategic plan for an event that are unique in comparison to those of other products. For example, after affirming their own mission, values and objectives of the event, the organization needs to analyze the community for event potential. They then must analyze the internal and external environment for factors that ensure or prevent success. This process is called a SWOT analysis, which stands for strengths, weaknesses, opportunities and threats. This process should be used to ensure the viability of the proposed event.

To write the marketing portion of the strategic plan considerable time must be spent analyzing what type of visitor will be most interested in attending the event. Research will most likely need to be conducted on the event preferences of the targeted visitors. After the visitor segment has been determined, the plan will address the details of the event including venue, staffing, entertainment, activities and vendors needed. A detailed agenda for planning purposes will need to be developed so all tasks are completed by the day of the event.

Financial issues including revenue sources, pricing and budgeting will also need to be decided. Revenue sources would be described including sponsorships along with the rationale for ticket pricing. A detailed budget will need to be part of the plan. The budget will include all expenses that will be incurred from marketing and implementing the event plan. The budget will also include all projected revenue sources. Because the final details on expenses and revenue cannot be known until after the event, this is called a projected or pro forma budget. After the event, the projected expense and revenue numbers will be compared to the actual.

Finally, marketing would need to be addressed. First, the marketing message including text, visuals and videos aimed at the segment of potential visitors would be described. Branding of the event theme will be explained. Then the means of communicating the message with both traditional and social media would be described. Finally, a detailed marketing plan will be included with how all communication methods, print, broadcast and social, will be used to attract attendance. In the appendix of the report would be a template that would detail the agenda for the day. This is crucial for the organization presenting the event to ensure that it runs smoothly with a minimum of problems.

The amount of work to develop this plan will depend on the size of the event. The larger and longer the event, the more time needs to be put into planning. It is critical that as many people as possible be involved in the planning process (Das 2019). Doing so builds enthusiasm as people want to feel a part of a larger goal rather than just doing daily tasks. It is then necessary to hold regular meetings to reinforce that the tasks people are assigned are being completed to ensure success of the day of the event.

Uses of event strategic plans

The strategic plan will be shown to potential partnership sponsors and other community organizations so they will understand that the event has a good chance for success. As a result, they will hopefully then be motivated to become involved. Lastly, a plan is needed that details how the promotional ideas will be implemented. This will be used internally and describe in detail the targeted visitor segment, the marketing message and the media that will be used to communicate. If the event is a success, the organization may decide to hold it again or even make it a recurring event. The same plan can be used with any needed adjustments. It will just need to be revamped based on what was learned from the first implementation of the plan.

Tourism officials planning events now understand they must go beyond simply providing an enjoyable experience. They must provide an experience that has activities that promote interaction between attendees but also between attendees and the local community. Those working in hospitality need to learn to partner in creating these experiences. The stay at the hotel must be part of the experience and not just a place to sleep.

For this reason, it is necessary to learn to understand how travelers' needs have changed, particularly since the use of social media to share experiences. They must learn how to access their communities so that they can offer the experiences that will be local authentic experiences. They must learn how to package these events using community organizations and individuals, not just tourism service providers. Finally, they must effectively market their events using both traditional and social media.

Finding ideas for events

Before designing an event to attract potential visitors it is necessary to analyze the surrounding community to determine what type of event can be developed. Events can be defined as a way of spending time away from home to pursue pleasurable or educational activities while making use of local products and services. The definition is so broad that it is up to those planning the event to define what activities, products and services will be promoted as part of the experience. Potential visitors put considerable effort into making the decision as to where to travel as the activities, products and services reinforce a current identity or create a new identity for the visitor. The suppliers of tourism products have always known this and have used marketing to encourage travel as a way to either get away to exclusive destinations or, for the mass market, to join the fun where everyone else was traveling to. Now tourism and hospitality organizations are responding to a newer trend of visitors using travel to interact with local culture and meet local community members.

Assessing the physical setting

An event is unique because it is a product composed of the physical setting of where it is held along with the experience that it provides. A successful event will reflect the authentic community in which it is being held rather than be a fantasy idea of what the community wishes to be (Hemmings 2018). The physical aspects of the event, such as the venue, along with the entertainment inside the venue, together create the attendance experience. The venue contains physical elements such as the architecture and design of the venue or public space in which it is taking place. It also includes the immediate environment surrounding the venue such as parks, streets and monuments. These physical features will be an important component in developing the event's image whether as an historical, sophisticated or a trend-setting event.

It is not just well-known cultural buildings that can be used as venues, though these will be of interest to visitors to events. Sites that are related to the history of specific religious or ethnic groups may also be of interest to visitors and can be used as venues. The places where sports teams play can be used as venues as they will attract sport fans. Even buildings and locations associated with films or literature can be used as venues that visitors may want to experience. The physical elements surrounding the venue that can be appealing to visitors also include the geographic setting of the community. Being located by a river, ocean or mountains adds to the value of experiencing the event. Both the venue and the physical setting of the venue together will be used to add to the event's attractiveness.

In the past, many communities would only focus their tourism marketing message on the venue for the event. They would promote the fact that it was being held in a large cultural institution or a venue such as a museum, historical site or sports arena. It was assumed that this would be all that was necessary to attract visitors. This might still be the case for world-renowned historical or cultural sites.

While there are few communities that are home to such institutions, all communities have examples of sites and buildings of local interest that can be used as venues that are attractive to visitors. It is not the venue, but the experience that the visitor will have that is the benefit that will be marketed (Finch 2019). There is so much choice in destinations that the potential visitor does not have the time to analyze what they will experience. The marketing message must clearly state the benefits of visiting the venue where the event is being held.

All communities trying to attract visitors to events also need to assess if they can provide the needed services. A larger city has an advantage in developing and marketing events. People are already traveling to large cities because they are regional, national or even international centers of commerce. Because this is true, they will already have businesses that provide food and lodging to visitors. In addition, they will have a transportation system to get to, and around, the city. It is easy for these cities simply to add more events to the calendar. Providing tourism services can be a challenge for small cities and towns as they may need to ensure that adequate transportation, lodging and food services for visitors are available.

Assessing the people

The built environment of a city is easiest to understand and catalogue as they are physical sites, monuments and buildings of which almost everyone is aware. They may be famous, such as a monument to those killed in a war, or known only to those in the community, such as the site of an historic market square. Both types are used by community members as reference points when giving directions as it is assumed that everyone knows where they are located. On a larger scale, and more difficult to understand, are districts or neighborhoods that share a distinction that makes them unique. Although outsiders may initially see the city as homogenous, locals know that there are distinctions based on ethnic or religious background, lifestyle or social class.

It is essential that before an event is developed, the residents in the community and the groups they represent are understood, and not just the physical environment. Recently there has been a change in preference in what people desire from the visitor experience from which smaller cities and town can benefit. While they still may want to visit well-known landmarks, they know that these sites do not reflect the daily cultural life of the community. It is this daily life that they want to experience and explore. While it can be easy to catalogue major physical sites and buildings, it is more difficult to analyze people and the local neighborhood culture.

The activities engaged in by local community members may not be thought of as being of interest to others because they are simply part of the lived experience of the community. However, local community members that practice skills tied to a different time period or culture will be of interest to visitors looking for authentic experiences. For example, as interest in the local food movement grows, visitors may be interested in meeting community members that tend large gardens and preserve their own food. Visitors with an interest in fiber arts may wish to learn more about weaving from a local resident.

This is also true of sharing stories of the origins of local customs. Visitors will remember their interactions with the local people they encounter just as much as what they have experienced at the event (Bettiol 2020). This is particularly true now that events can be experienced online without visiting. It is the local residents that can only be encountered through a visit that are a motivation for visiting that cannot be duplicated online. Local residents, who sit in cafés talking about the old days with each other, can find a new audience with visitors who are eager to listen. The heritage, interests and friendliness of the people are now part of the event product and should be assessed and promoted.

Determining the central event theme

Every event must have a central theme or core product around which all the event activities and entertainment are connected. There are many choices for this central theme. Tourism organizations can develop a plan built around already existing cultural and sports events. First, professional performing arts organizations might be the central theme or core. A larger city might have established theater, dance and music companies with reputations that will already draw in visitors. The next step would be to design an event around one or more of these cultural organizations. The same can be done with museums. The event core is the museum with various other activities added to attract visitors. Major sporting venues already attract visitors. An event could be built around the venue to increase visitation and attract a new visitor segment

Smaller communities may not have these types of established cultural attractions or sport venues. Instead of having professional companies they can build an event around amateur performances that also allow the visitor to participate in some way. If there is a local sport, the same can be done by teaching visitors the rules of the game. Smaller communities can also build events around local history and culture. Finally, smaller communities can focus on attracting a segment of visitors interested in an interest or hobby around which an event is built. Another common theme for events is the type of food and drink specific to the local community. All kinds of communities can develop events around these categories.

Traditional tourism strategy has been to focus on events involving performances or sporting events that are well known and will draw in a large number of tourists. Smaller events based on local cultural heritage were thought to have a low appeal to visitors. This has now changed as more people are interested in local, small-scale events. Concerns with health issues have also resulted in people seeking out events that are closer to home rather than at a distance.

Analysis process of event potential

Developing a tourism event first involves determining what event core product will be offered. This is the main motivation for attending the event whether it is a music concert, history reenactment or food festival. Because of social media the potential visitor is aware of many similar events from which they can choose. When searching online the visitor will be looking for not just an event but a total experience which consists of the core product and then other activities. These activities that allow for participation and are themed to the main event are called supporting products. Not all events may include every idea for additional entertainment, education, shopping and refreshments. However as many as appropriate should be added if they can be themed to the core event.

To learn what additional supporting activities can be added, an in-depth analysis of the community's core and supporting product needs to be conducted so that the event will motivate attendance while accurately reflecting the authentic community. This analysis should be conducted by staff members along with volunteers from the community.

Having staff and community members work together on the analysis has the advantage of having the staff members become very knowledgeable on all aspects of the city while local residents become more supportive of the event.

The first step will be for a committee of staff members and volunteers to assess what they believe are the main features that could be developed into an event that would attract visitors. This process should be interesting, as everyone will bring differing opinions as to what the city has to offer.

The event potential analysis would include all local tourist attractions. These are businesses that have been established for the express purpose of providing entertainment to visitors. However, community non-profit organizations, which include arts and cultural organizations, universities and colleges, and even churches, should be included as they may also provide attractions and events of interest to visitors. At this point in the process, it should be understood that all event ideas should be included. Later, the ideas will be prioritized, with the most likely to succeed being chosen.

Cultural events potential

When the word culture is mentioned many people immediately think of the fine arts. However, when analyzing the community, tourism officials need to consider culture in a much broader context. The cultural environment includes the physical representations of culture such as heritage or historical sites, history museums, churches, the architectural style of buildings, historic homes and monuments. However, it also includes the cultural heritage that is represented by ethnic communities or organizations.

The planned event might be focused on cultural attributes such as the visual arts. The committee will certainly consider as part of the core event product the paintings and objects that can be enjoyed in museums or galleries. However, any public art, including civic and funeral monuments, should also be included in the analysis as these could be the focus of hosted walking tours. The performing arts are also an important part of the core event product that can be enjoyed by visitors. The city may provide the opportunity to listen to various types of live music including classical, folk, rock, popular or ethnic. The opportunity to experience dance might also be provided to visitors through performances of ballet, modern or ethnic dance. Also included in the analysis should be opportunities to enjoy theatre including popular or serious plays, musicals and variety shows. All of these cultural opportunities may be presented by professional organizations. However, local amateur companies can also provide tourists with an enjoyable experience.

The living heritage of a city can be difficult to assess because it is so woven into the fabric of the community. As a result, it may not be considered unique, simply because it is what members of the community experience every day. However, a desire to experience this unique living heritage can motivate visitors to attend an event. The living heritage would include the community's handicrafts, religion, occupational history, ethnic groups, languages, unique customs, and festivals. Even the city's industrial past is also part of its living heritage. The committee assessing event potential should consider all of these examples of the heritage as something that can potentially be the core of an event.

Entertainment and sports event potential

Entertainment can be the event core product or be additional activities. Entertainment opportunities include going to movies, dance clubs, and bars and pubs. The event might also use entertainment to provide additional activities that tourists will enjoy, including open mic nights, karaoke signing or dance lessons. The venues at which this entertainment might take place include hotels, restaurants, bars, building lobbies, parks and even retail establishments. If sufficiently available, sports viewing or participation may also be found to be part of a city's core product. In addition, an analysis of retail businesses and the products they offer will also be needed as unique shopping opportunities may be a reason for visiting the event. While it is increasingly difficult to make the distinction between what is considered art and what is considered entertainment, the city does not need to worry about the distinction when planning events. The event can provide a menu of cultural and entertainment opportunities from which the visitor can choose.

Central event themes

- Tourist attractions: Theme park, zoos, museums.
- Cultural organizations: Theatre groups, music groups, art galleries.
- Ethnic: Cultural associations, local food specialties, ethnic festivals.
- Universities: Architecture, theater groups, student galleries.
- Religious: Temples, churches or synagogues, shrines, sites of religious significance.
- Historical sites: Homes of famous people, sites of battles.
- Natural: Landscapes, parks, gardens, wilderness.
- Shopping: Unique retail, craft stores, discount shopping.

Analyzing available supporting products and services

This next step in the event analysis process will be to analyze what other products and services will be needed to support the event. The core event attraction alone may not be enough to motivate visitors. The process of analyzing a city for event potential is complex, as there may be multiple core event possibilities depending on the visitor segment that is targeted. In fact, the same city may contain more than one event potential, each of which may be attractive to a different group of potential visitors. For example, the city might have the resources and setting to develop an outdoor summer classical music festival that is attended by music lovers. In addition, the same city might also provide a core product of a transportation museum that is attractive to train fans all year round. The decision must then be made if there are enough staff and financial resources to develop two events or only to focus on developing one.

Total event experience

It may be the availability of supporting products that decides which event idea to develop. Supporting products are those that enhance the visitor's enjoyment of the main event. Some of the supporting products offered to visitors will be unique to each event. For example, the music lovers attending the summer concerts may also desire to purchase digital recordings of their favorite performing group while the train buffs will want to buy books on the history of the railroad. Another supporting product that a visitor might also purchase are tours specifically geared toward the home of a famous composer or the local railroad station.

Both tourist segments, no matter if they are visiting for the concerts or for the museum, will also need other general tourism supporting products. These supporting products include the essential tourist support services of food, lodging and transportation. Also needed are services that are optional such as car rental, medical care, religious services and general tours and souvenirs of the area.

Food and refreshment availability

Visitors attending the event will need restaurant and dining facilities that are conveniently located, clean and well maintained. Visitors to events will be interested in restaurants that offer locally grown food or have local specialties on the menu. The price range of the restaurants that will be promoted as part of the event should fit what the targeted visitor segment would be willing to spend. In small communities it may be necessary to convince the restaurant owners to be open the days and hours needed by visitors.

Since food is a basic necessity for all visitors, the analysis for an event should include compiling a list of all types of restaurants, whether a fine-dining opportunity or a food truck. Because this cataloguing process requires only routine research using online sources or visiting establishments, it is a task that could be undertaken by any staff member or even a volunteer. The routine information obtained should include the name of the establishment, website and social media accounts, hours, phone number and address and name of the owner or manager. It should also include information on the type of establishment, the menu, the clientele and cost.

Once this information is compiled it can be analyzed by the committee to determine if there is a sufficient number and range of establishments that fit the theme of the event and will be attractive to the targeted visitor segment. Hopefully there are sufficient establishments to provide visitors with the opportunity to have breakfast, lunch, dinner and even a late-night snack. It is especially important that there should be menu options and prices to match the expectations of the targeted visitor segment. For example, while expensive fine dining might be enjoyed by one visitor segment, if the event is targeted at families there needs to be restaurants where the family can have an inexpensive breakfast.

The food establishments can then be analyzed for any unique concepts that can be marketed to visitors. For example, the community may have a number of restaurants that fall into a certain category such as ethnic food, fine dining or family style that can then be promoted as supporting a specific core event. For example, ethnic food restaurants could be packaged with an ethnic arts festival.

Lodging availability

Visitors to events who are staying overnight will also need the supporting service of lodging. The issue that needs to be analyzed is if there are sufficient lodging establishments to meet the needs of the targeted visitor segment. In addition, does the price range fit in with what visitors would be willing to pay. An analysis might find that there are facilities that need improvement because they are not well maintained and should not be promoted until the problems are corrected. If the event is targeting a market segment that is not interested in staying in a traditional hotel or motel, it must be discovered if there are any alternative forms of lodging available.

The analysis of available lodging will be an easier process than that of food establishments, as there will be fewer businesses to catalogue and analyze. While hotels and motels should be included in the analysis, alternative lodging opportunities including bed and breakfast establishments, long-term-stay apartment facilities, rooms in private residences, and youth hostels should also be included. In addition, the city may provide campgrounds, RV parks and short-term rentals of private homes.

The information to be catalogued should include the name of the establishment, address and contact information, clientele, service, style and the cost of the establishment. The lodging should be then analyzed for any additional services it offers that would be attractive to the visitor segment that is being targeted with the event core product. This information on lodging, besides being an essential part of product analysis, can be useful in other ways. It should be provided on the event social media and website. In addition, the list can be analyzed to determine what food establishments and lodging to package with the core product to promote to different visitor groups.

Transportation needs

Often forgotten when analyzing the event supporting product is the city's transportation system. It also needs to be analyzed as to its adequacy and ease of use for visitors. If it is unique, the transportation system can even be a core event product in itself. The transportation needs of visitors should include the airport, bus and train stations. If visitors are driving, the availability of adequate and reasonably priced parking facilities near the event venue or hotels needs be addressed. Another issue to consider is if there are walking and bike paths for visitors who don't drive, and local transportation around the city so that the visitor can easily get to attractions and events.

The availability of other services that might be needed by visitors, which may not come immediately to mind, should be catalogued. These include services such as emergency medical care, food to meet special dietary needs, religious services, late-night pharmacies, childcare and police assistance. While this information will not become part of the promotional message for the city, compiling this list will still be of use. The information obtained on the availability of the services, including what establishment offers the service, where it is located, contact information, and the days and hours it is available, can be posted online and also printed into a brochure that is available at the event and in participating hotels. Even if the visitor does not need the information, it is just another means of making the visitor feel welcome.

Tours and souvenirs

There should be an analysis of any tours designed for specific interest groups that may be attending. For example, a music festival might offer a tour at a local museum with an exhibit of historical instruments. A festival focused on a cultural group could also offer tours of the local ethnic community. People attending the event will also want to bring home products as souvenirs. There should be an analysis to determine if there are products that would be of interest to the targeted visitor segment. Hopefully, as much as possible these souvenirs should be locally made and available to purchase in different price ranges.

Other event components

- Restaurants: Type of food, price range, local specialties.
- Lodging: Type, price range, alternative lodging.
- Transportation: Bus, train, bikes, parking.

- Other: Childcare, emergency medical, religious services.
- Souvenirs: General, locally made, specific to community.
- Tours: General walking tours, museum tours, history tours, ghost tours.

Discussion questions

1. What types of event planning needs to be done to ensure success?
2. What sites and experiences in your community can be packaged as an event?
3. How should an analysis of the community's core event potential be done?
4. Why is the first impression the city makes to visitors critical?
5. What are some ideas for core event themes in a community?
6. Why should food establishments be analyzed by visitor segment?
7. Why should lodging be analyzed by theme?
8. What types of transportation should be analyzed?

Case

The community is the event

Berea, Kentucky in the United States is part of Appalachia, a mountainous and isolated area where many traditional forms of craft were maintained by the people because they could not afford to purchase mass-produced goods. They were into sustainability before it became a trendy concept. The city is home to Berea College, whose mission is to provide education to students from Appalachia with limited financial means. One of the unique features of the college is its focus on students learning traditional crafts, such as woodworking, weaving and broom making. Not only do students learn the heritage of the area, the products produced are sold as a means of raising revenue.

So how does the city of Berea, with an isolated location and a population of less than 15,000 attract visitors? They knew there were people interested in sustainability and traditional crafts. So they used the unique culture of the area to package family-friendly learning opportunities through the Festival of Learnshops held each summer. Classes, all taught by local artisans, are offered on such skills as blacksmithing, gourd art, basketmaking and learning to play the dulcimer. The experience is more than just classes. The festival is packaged as a way to experience the culture of Appalachia. Visitors can:

- Explore the historic town while buying crafts produced by local artists.
- Stay in the college-owned historic Boone Tavern Inn staffed by students.
- Eat at restaurants serving local foods such as spoonbread.
- Join jam sessions with local musicians playing traditional instruments.

This event didn't just happen. It was actively supported by the city government as a means of not only increasing tourism revenue but also increasing the income of local artists and musicians that teach the lessons and sell their products. The city provides the space for the classes, festival marketing and insurance coverage. They have even offered a two-day workshop for artists and musicians to improve their business skills. Every community has people with unique skills that they can share (Moses 2016).

Task: Determine what type of skills community members can share with visitors.

Case

Connecting people at virtual events

We all know someone who excels at navigating a crowded networking event. For these extroverts, going into a crowded event where they don't know anyone is just like going on holiday. For introverts, it is more like a trip to the dentist! Introverts also are not comfortable with posing questions, not wishing to be intrusive.

Virtual events can make networking easier for the many introverts who want to make contact at events but find it difficult to do so. Introverts enjoy a one-to-one conversation where information is exchanged rather than casual chitchat while trying to simultaneously balance a plate and a glass of wine. Virtual events have the following advantages.

- Virtual events allow attendees to be polled about with whom they wish to connect.
- Virtual chat rooms can then be set up where conversations can be held without distraction.
- During virtual presentations, they can present questions electronically with a moderator fielding and submitting questions to the presenter.

We all know that most question periods at in-person events are often dominated by the same few people who consider themselves smarter than the presenter. Virtual events can level the playing field and allow everyone equal opportunity to present. As a result, new voices heard and new ideas presented (Ancowitz 2020)!

Task: Decide how part of your event could be shared virtually with people unable to attend.

Event plan: Use the information from this chapter to complete the first section of the event plan outline at the end of the book.

References

Ancowitz, Nancy. 2020. "Zounds! We Are on Zoom: Introverts Can Lead Virtually." *Psychology Today.* March 24, 2020. https://www.psychologytoday.com/us/blog/self-promotion-introverts/202003/zounds-we-re-zoom-introverts-can-lead-virtually-0. Accessed August 5, 2020.

Bettiol, Claudia. 2020. "How to Promote Tourism in 5 Strategic Steps." *DiscoverPlaces. Travel.* August 27, 2020. https://discoverplaces.travel/en/how-to-promote-tourism-in-5-strategic-steps-2/. Accessed October 13, 2020.

Das, Pritom. 2019. "5 Actionable Strategic-Planning Tips to Boost Business Efficiency." *Entrepreneur.* November 4, 2019. https://www.entrepreneur.com/article/341784. Accessed October 26, 2020.

Finch, Susan. 2019. "7 Tourism Marketing Challenges and How to Overcome Them. *SF Gate.* June 26, 2019. https://marketing.sfgate.com/blog/tourism-marketing-challenges. Accessed November 14, 2020.

Hemmings, Laura. 2018. "The Importance of Community in Event." *We Are Placemaking.* March 12, 2018. https://www.weareplacemaking.co.uk/importance-of-community-in-events/. Accessed November 7, 2020.

Moses, E. 2016. Arts and the Economy: A Perfect Match for Kentucky Communities. *Kentucky Leagues of Cities.* Available from: *klc.org.* http://www.klc.org/UserFiles/Arts_and_economy.pdf. Accessed March 18, 2016.

Chapter 3

Determining event goals and objectives

Abstract

Gaining the support of the community during the event planning process is critical to success. Visitors want to interact with the community as this is part of the event experience. The community must support the event and welcome visitors while government officials need to help with easing any restrictions. Civic groups and businesses owners will be critical to providing visitors with experiences and services. Economic and sociocultural trends, and technology, will affect the strategic decisions that need to be made. The mission of the organization is the reason that it exists while the values explain the larger role the organization plays in the community. The mission and values of the organizations that are creating the event will be scrutinized by visitors to see if they are relevant and if they are followed. A SWOT analysis analyzes the internal strengths and weaknesses of the organization. It also analyzes the external opportunities and threats. From this information, objectives and tasks will be developed.

Assessing community support and internal resources

Creating a strategy for the development and marketing of a tourism event should involve the entire community as they are part of the event product. Visitors to a tourism event will affect the daily life of the community. While it might bring in needed revenue, it will also bring crowds which can be inconvenient, causing traffic and noise. The process of community involvement in the planning process should address the concerns that the event will harm more than help the community. Getting the support of key stakeholders such as local residents, business leaders, civic associations and government officeholders at the start of the planning process will be critical to success.

Community concerns

To be successful, the development plan for the event must have the support of key stakeholder groups in the community whether or not they will be actively involved. The common concerns of overcrowding of local establishments and higher prices caused by tourism will be expressed by some community residents, but the use of social media to share information on destinations now brings a new concern. One of the arguments that may be raised by community members against holding the event is that bringing in visitors will spread a negative perception of the community. This is because social media allows visitors to communicate their own messages about the city. It may be that what visitors share online is not how the local community wishes to be known (Roy 2019). It may even be information on aspects of the city or stories of local residents of which the residents are not proud.

The use of social media has another effect on communities. Even when social media comments are positive, problems can result. Positive comments about community amenities can destroy exactly what makes the city attractive. Comments on social media can turn what were community amenities, such as riverfront parks, into tourism products. While previously these amenities may have been enjoyed only by community members, once discovered online they will now be shared with visitors. Even everyday experiences, such as neighbors having overnight visitors, can become commercial transactions that are part of the tourism industry when these visitors become paying guests. While financially rewarding for the homeowner, the activity may not be welcomed by neighbors.

Community and government support

Larger communities may already have a convention and visitor bureau or a destination marketing organization that is responsible for marketing events to potential visitors. In contrast, small communities may have to rely on only a single paid marketer and a visitor center staffed by volunteers. In either case the development of a tourism event cannot be developed alone by staff. Instead staff should make use of community members interested in developing event tourism as they can bring fresh insights and ideas for activities to the process. The stakeholders that might be involved include community members, government officials, civic groups, business organizations and creative entrepreneurs.

Starting the process of the development of an event strategic plan without getting the support of key stakeholder groups can lead to resentment and opposition to the plan. Because the continuing support of these community groups is critical to the success of any event development effort, it is essential that the level of community support for the event tourism be assessed on an ongoing basis. Tourism officials may carefully develop an event plan that includes local activities and services. However, this same plan will fail if those who are responsible for providing visitors with the needed activities services are not willing to enthusiastically do so.

Increasing support through involvement

To optimize success, as many community groups should be involved in the process of developing a tourism event as possible. First, the people who will provide the already available products and services to visitors should be involved as they must be willing to actively join in marketing efforts, particularly those involving social media. This is necessary as visitors will want to communicate directly with community members to schedule an authentic local experience (Stavans and Ellison 2015). It is only through direct contact with potential visitors that these desires will become known. Local creative entrepreneurial individuals and organizations should be involved as they have the ability to provide new products and services that are currently not being offered. While they can provide the ideas and energy, they may need guidance on how to position the new products as part of the experience of the event. Finally, members of the community not directly related to tourism need to be involved as if they are not supportive, they can harm the effort to develop the event by not welcoming visitors online or in person.

Government officials need to be involved in the development of tourism as they control resources that will be needed for developing and marketing the event. Unless they understand the benefits that the event will bring to the community, they may be unwilling to grant any needed permits and other support. With the growth of services such as Airbnb for lodging and Uber for transportation, the role of government becomes even more critical. Many communities are grappling with whether or how to regulate these on-demand economy businesses. Having a good working relationship with government officials will mean that all voices will be heard when these decisions are made.

Civic groups and business owners

Civic organizations will also need to participate in developing a tourism event plan. This would include such groups as social clubs, historical societies and cultural organizations. All of these already have experience in attracting members or visitors and can share their expertise. In addition, they can all benefit from additional visitors to the community. Social clubs that represent cultural groups need to be included as they may be interested in providing the authentic experience that visitors desire. Historical associations may not have a direct link with tourism but may offer activities that can attract visitors from outside the area. Cultural organizations, whether focused on fine art or local culture, will be of interest to visitors wanting to have authentic experiences. None of these groups may be currently thinking of visitors as part of their mission. They may need encouragement to see how their mission can be expanded by event tourism as it will expose new visitors to local culture.

The last group that needs to be involved are local business owners. It might be assumed that they would be natural allies of the effort to increase tourism. For example, business owners, especially those that provide products and services needed by visitors, should be motivated by self-interest to support the idea of developing the event. Some business people may fear that increasing tourism will attract new businesses to the area, thereby increasing competition. Even if they are supportive, they may need to learn how to adapt their product and customer service to what is desired and expected by visitors.

Business associations, such as a Chamber of Commerce, would also fall into this category. Since one of the reasons for their existence is to promote business, they should be natural supporters of event tourism efforts as some visitors may decide to relocate to the community. An area without any current ties to tourism may still have a group that is tasked with economic development. The local economic development authority may also be supportive as they are aware that increasing tourism may result in new businesses relocating from somewhere else. Finally, individual entrepreneurs might be willing to join the effort to provide products and experiences the community currently lacks.

Government agencies

Before starting to create an event, the organizations involved need to determine if they have the necessary financial resources and staff with the necessary skills needed to turn an event idea into a successful reality. While the event may generate revenue from ticket sales, sponsorships and products from the event, there will be money that needs to be spent during the planning period for expenses such as rental fees for facilities, deposits to caterers and promotional expenses that will need to be covered. If the organization does not have money to cover these expenses, it must be found from government sources, grants from community organizations or fronted by for-profit businesses. Without the needed funds in hand, event planning should not take place.

One source for these funds might be economic development agencies with a mission of attracting and supporting businesses to the area. They may understand the tourism events are a way to introduce people to the area who may then decide to relocate their business. These types of agencies can be housed in a number of different government offices and organizations. One of the most common is a redevelopment agency, which is formed by municipal governments to provide grants and loans. While advice is wonderful, it is often cash that is needed. Here, economic development authorities can help by providing the needed startup funds.

In 2019 globally tourism was 10 percent of GDP which is three times larger than agriculture (Constantin, Saxon and Yu 2020). Because of the importance of tourism, a variety of different government agencies may be a source of funding. Transport agencies may be able to assist with funding to provide environmentally friendly transport options. Health agencies may be interested in helping cover the costs of ensuring that everyone at the event stays healthy. Departments dedicated to sports are also a source of funding.

Groups needed to support the event

- Community: Welcome visitors.
- Government: Because of regulatory issues and funding.
- Civic groups: Activities and attributes they can share.
- Business owners: Provide tourism services.

Assessing internal organizational resources

Personnel will also be needed for planning and staffing the event. Hopefully, current employees will have the necessary skills but, if not, either additional staff will need to be hired or the work will need to be outsourced. While doing so will cost money, not doing so may result in a failed event. First, there are highly skilled tasks for which the organization may lack someone with the needed skills, such as accounting. Most small organizations will need someone else to do their accounting, even if they must pay to have it done, because no one in the organization has the necessary skill. Second, the organization can outsource specialized tasks. For example, the organization might also hire a specialist to create marketing materials. Paying these service providers will still save money because, by hiring them, it frees the organization to spend time developing the event. Lastly, there are routine repetitive tasks that need to be done by someone who concentrates on their performance. Because these tasks are all that they do, such as responding to ticket requests, they can perform them more efficiently. It is possible that routine tasks might be handled by interns from a nearby educational institution or volunteers from a community organization.

Assessing external trends

It may be obvious that an organization developing a tourism event needs information about their community and also their available funding and staffing resources. It may be less obvious that time must be spent on analyzing external trends that influence if a person decides they have the money and interest that will motivate attendance at the event. Three of the main external trends where changes need to be analyzed are economic, sociocultural and technological. These trends, which are external to the organization, will also affect what type of event will have the best chance of success.

Economic influences

While an individual may be able to ignore the economic news, those working in tourism and hospitality must understand the current economic situation as it will affect how much disposable income potential visitors will have. Most people will only spend money on travel after they have paid for the basic needs of food, clothing and shelter. While it is true that when the economy is in decline consumer spending decreases and when the economy is growing consumer spending increases, the relationship is more complicated (Glassman 2019). A slowing economy does not immediately affect money spent on travel. It will not do so until members of the public believe the decline will be long lasting, and the same is true of economic expansion.

If the economy is doing poorly, it does not mean that no events should be planned. However it might be necessary to adjust prices or increase marketing to explain the value of attendance. In addition, if the economy is growing the price of event components such as catering, entertaining and the cost of renting venues might rise because of increased demand.

An online search of a government database should provide information on the current rate of economic growth. However, while a single number alone, such as the rate of economic growth, is data, it does not provide information. For example, the rate of economic growth in the region might be found to be 2.5 percent. This number can only be judged to be good or bad if the past percentages are known. For example, if growth had been at 4.2 percent the previous year, then 2.5 percent means that growth has slowed down significantly, and people may be concerned about retaining their jobs and, as a result, save money rather than spend. On the other hand, if economic growth has been at only 1.0 percent the previous year, the same 2.5 percent growth may make people feel the economy is recovering, and they will be more likely to spend money.

Of course, it is easier to attract visitors during times of economic prosperity when people have enough disposable income to travel. However, even during times when the economy is doing poorly, people can still be motivated to attend an event. There are people who will still have enough disposable income to travel, but to motivate them to do so the marketing plan must be adjusted to respond to the psychological effect of economic bad news. For example, the promotion for the event can focus on the low cost of attendance as compared with other more expensive events. If this is not true, then a special promotional package with lower pricing may need to be developed and promoted. In fact, if tourists can be offered lower costs, the poor state of the economy may be an opportunity to attract tourists away from more expensive travel options. Understanding how the economy is performing will assist event organizers in adjusting their promotional efforts to address the economic concerns of potential visitors.

Social and cultural influences

The social and cultural environment influences a person's choice of where to travel, when to travel and with whom to travel. Among the social factors that are important to marketing an event are people's values and their chosen lifestyle. Event organizers must analyze the values and lifestyles of targeted visitors as they directly affect the choice of event to attend.

Lifestyle is a term that refers to the wide range of choices people make on how they want to spend their time, the products they purchase and consume, and with whom they wish to associate. In previous generations, occupation, income and social class mostly established lifestyle. For instance, in many countries if a person was a doctor, they had a high income and belonged to an upper social class. As a result they were expected to maintain a certain lifestyle. Meanwhile manual workers had lower incomes, were considered to belong to a different social class and would have their own lifestyle. Marketers could target people by grouping them on the closely related factors of occupation, income and social class, and design a marketing plan based on an assumption of how each group spent their time, what they wanted to consume and with whom they wished to associate.

However, people now tend to define themselves more by lifestyle choice rather than by their occupation and social class. Tourism marketers should target potential visitors by lifestyle choice rather than just demographic characteristics. For example, both the doctor and the manual worker may be interested in biking, cooking or nightlife. Social listening, which refers to monitoring social media sites, is a way to learn about lifestyle choices. Simply going online to find out the latest hashtags can provide ideas for what activities may be popular.

An example of how new lifestyles can provide an opportunity for events is the growth in interest in extreme sports. Cities located near wilderness areas now can develop an event to attract this new group of tourists. Another example is the interest in yoga. Communities that do not have outstanding scenery or architecture could promote an event focused on healthy living. By being aware of lifestyle changes tourism event marketers can develop an event that responds to either the opportunity or challenge presented.

Cultural values are strongly held, enduring beliefs about how life should be lived. These values will also affect the attendance decision. For example, an increasing emphasis on family values may result in more families wishing to attend events together. If tourism marketers want to take advantage of this value shift by developing events for families, they must include in their promotional material information on children's activities and their educational value. Another value held by many people is the importance of the natural world. To attract visitors holding this value, an event built around the city's parks, waterways, bike paths and nearby outdoor recreational activities could be promoted.

Many people value the past by holding an idealized view of small-town or village life. Many smaller cities can benefit from this nostalgia by emphasizing their own charm and friendliness to attract visitors to heritage events. Of course, groups of people will also hold cultural values that pertain to national origin or ethnic group and these also must be considered. If an international market segment is being targeted, it is important to understand their own national values and to adjust the event theme and activities accordingly.

Social concerns, and cultural identity, are critical to analyze as they affect people's event preferences. People are increasingly forming part of their identity around social issues that have meaning to them. Social media can be used to analyze the issues that are of concern. Simply following Twitter can provide information (Ahmed 2019). The social issue might be a concern for environmental issues that results in visitors wishing to attend events that do not harm the environment. Another social issue might be poverty, which might result in visitors wishing to attend events that assist in local economic development. Sociocultural issues can also include purchasing behaviors based on customers' ethnic origins, which affect their cultural identity. The differing roles of men and women, the importance of children, and the attitude toward the elderly will affect event choice. As the ethnicity of communities changes, event organizers must adapt and offer the desired events. For example, ethnic groups that wish to socialize as a family will not be interested in late-night performances.

Technological influences

Technological advancements can affect what people expect from an event. Adding technology to an event, such as social media walls, provides additional benefits desirable to the visitor. Technology also affects how the event is promoted. The ability to maintain direct communication between the event attender and the public has redefined promotion methods. For example, tweeting during the event should be encouraged as this aids promotion.

Technological changes can also have a negative on the event (Chrisos 2019). When an organization is dependent on technology for tasks, if the technology fails problems can result that will affect the success of an event. For example, if the electronic payment system for processing credit cards fails, the event cannot sell tickets. Another problem that results from technology is that employees who mostly communicate online may not have the interpersonal social skills to make visitors feel welcome. In addition, event staff from different organizations that only interact with each other using technology may not develop the personal relationships needed to be able to work together on event projects.

External influences

- Economic influences: Money to spend.
- Social and cultural: Travel decisions.
- Technological expectations: Types of experiences.

Mission and values

All organizations, including tourism, lodging and event-related businesses, have missions that incorporate the reason they exist. For businesses, their mission is to provide a product or service that is needed or desired by a group of consumers. To meet their mission, any business will want to produce the very best product that they can at a price that is affordable for their targeted customers. A mission for an event is similar: it is the reason it is being held. Those designing the event will want to provide a superior experience at a price affordable for the targeted visitor segment. What differs is that the mission for an event is broader. The event will also provide benefits to the community as a whole.

Organizational mission

Consumers make a purchase decision not just by product features or price but also based on the mission of the organization (Ferrell et al. 2019). Therefore, included in mission statements should be information on how the event will improve the local or wider community. All organizations must meet their missions with limited resources. Too broad a mission will result in organizational resources being spread too thinly, with the danger that nothing will be achieved.

There is a basic difference in the missions of for-profit businesses and tourism organizations when trying to design and promote an event. If a for-profit company discovers that the product they produce is no longer wanted by consumers, they will change their mission and produce something that is desired. Because tourism organizations have a responsibility to their communities, they may be unwilling to create events based only the fact that will draw the most visitors. This means that they will need to design events that both attract visitors and benefit the community. They will then use promotion to carefully target those visitors who will appreciate what the community has to offer.

The statement for a tourism event should first explain what it does or the reason for its existence. It might state that their mission is to provide a weekend craft festival focused on basketmaking. Next the statement would explain who is to benefit, which would be that the craft festival will provide an opportunity for local residents to share their skill while visitors from the outside the area will have an enjoyable and educational experience. The last part of the mission statement, or why, is the lasting benefit that results. It might state that the event will provide a positive spotlight on the community, bring needed economic benefits and bond families through shared activities.

Organizational values

An organization is more than just its mission. Organizations, just like individuals, also have values. Values, deep-seated beliefs about what actions are right and just, will affect how the mission is implemented. People expect a mission statement to contain ethical standards (Pawinska Sims 2018). Each organization's value statement will be unique. While challenging to write, such statements can provide guidance in making the many choices when organizing an event. For example, the organizational value might be to make the event environmentally sustainable. When the organizations involved in planning the event need to make decisions, such as what type of venue to use and food to serve, the value statement will assist in the decision-making process.

SWOT analysis

After analyzing the community, the internal resources and the external environment, the organization will have a large quantity of interesting information. The question is how to make sense of all the data. One tool that can help to do this is the SWOT analysis, which stands for strengths, weaknesses, opportunities and threats. The information on internal resources will be analyzed to determine if it includes strengths, such as available funds for promotion, or weaknesses, such as lack of marketing knowledge. However, the distinction between something being a strength or weakness is not always so clear (Brandenburger 2019). For example, while an organization may determine that the community has a lack of luxury lodging choices, this is not a weakness if the visitors they are targeting are families on a budget. The determination of whether the presence or lack of a resource is a strength or weakness depends on the goals of the event.

Opportunities and threats are determined from the information uncovered in the analysis of the economic, sociocultural and economic external environment. For example, an analysis of the economic situation might have discovered a demand for shorter trips, closer to home. This provides an opportunity to target nearby communities with promotional messages about the low cost of travel to the event. An analysis of the sociocultural environment might also have found a newly arrived ethnic community that has settled in the area. This might be an opportunity to target them as potential visitors to an ethnic festival. Another example of an external change might be learning that many residents are concerned about safety and health. If this is true, and if the event is being held outdoors, then there is an opportunity to target people who are concerned about being inside a crowded enclosed space. Threats may also be uncovered when analyzing the economic environment. If it is learned that economic growth is low and unemployment high, the threat is that potential customers will not be able to afford to travel. The answer is not for the organization to stop having events but rather to either lower the price or develop a promotional message that explains why attending the event is worth the price.

Objectives and tasks

The purpose of the SWOT analysis is to understand the organization's internal strengths and then match the strength with an external opportunity. This match would then be stated in terms of a goal. A common saying is that a goal without a plan is a dream. For this reason the goals should be specific and quantifiable (Fresch 2019). A goal that is a general statement such as "provide an enjoyable experience" or "bring in more revenue" doesn't provide any information as to how to achieve the goal or to measure its success. A specific goal would be "provide an enjoyable experience so that the satisfaction rate of the post-event survey increases 10 per cent" or "bring in more revenue by increasing sales of food and beverage by 25 percent."

The next step would be to determine the objectives needed to accomplish the goal. Each objective is then broken down into what tasks need to be completed to meet the objective. It is completing the tasks that will make the goal a reality. Each objective might require more than one task for completion. The event plan will usually state the goals in terms of the event components that will be need to be implemented. An example, which is far from complete, is shown below.

Examples of a goal, objectives and tasks

Goal: Plan an ethnic festival for young families from local area.

- Objective 1: Find 20 local restaurants/civic groups to participate.
  Task: Contact restaurants to sign up.
  Task: Visit local civic groups to gauge interests.

- Objective 2: Provide three different dance demonstrations and lessons.
  Task: Contact local dance studio for classes.
  Task: Find dance floor to rent.
- Objective 3: Promote the event using five different social media methods.
  Task: Develop marketing message.
  Task: Create social media sites.

While a larger community with several tourism organizations and lodging choices may have many events planned, a smaller community with limited resources should only plan a single event. Once the event is a success, then additional events can be added.

The SWOT process

Conducting an effective SWOT analysis requires information, people and time. The information required will have already been obtained from conducting an internal analysis of the organization and the community. The analysis of the external economic, sociocultural and technological environments will also have provided information. The people required to complete a SWOT include a moderator and the involvement of enthusiastic staff and community members. If the SWOT analysis is to be successful, enough time must be allotted so that everyone can express their ideas. The purpose of the SWOT is not to just create lists but rather to answer questions (Gorny 2018). What external opportunities can be matched with internal strengths? Are there internal weaknesses that need to be addressed or can they be ignored? How can external threats be minimized? These are questions that will be answered during a SWOT analysis.

Before the SWOT analysis is conducted, the information obtained from the community and environmental scanning should be summarized into one document that is then distributed electronically to all committee members who will be involved. The reason for distributing the document before the SWOT analysis takes place is so that all those participating will have time to read the information and start to develop their own ideas on what type of event might be successful. The committee members can then come prepared to the SWOT analysis with some preliminary thoughts on opportunities and threats their event idea may confront.

The SWOT should be held at a convenient location with comfortable seating, tables for working and the necessary supplies. Refreshments should also be provided. Once at the SWOT analysis meeting the moderator should explain that everyone is encouraged to participate and that all ideas and opinions are welcome. A simple but effective means of obtaining people's ideas is to brainstorm. The moderator should ask everyone for their opinions on what they perceive as the community's strengths that can be used as the basis for developing an event. These ideas may be based on either their preexisting personal opinions or they may be new ideas that resulted from reading the report that was provided. During the brainstorming process it is the moderator's responsibility to ensure that, even though the discussion may become lively, there is no censoring of opinions.

At this stage in the process it is important to get everyone's ideas no matter how improbable or impracticable they may seem at first. The moderator's role is to make sure that everyone is heard but that no one person dominates the conversation. The committee members' ideas on strengths can be listed on large pieces of paper that are then posted about the room for everyone to see and consider. The same process is then repeated for determining weaknesses that might keep the event from becoming successful.

SWOT

- Strengths and weaknesses: Resources internal to organization that they control.
- Opportunities and threats: External forces to which the organization must react.

Reaching group consensus

After lists of event ideas have been created, the committee is now ready for consensus and prioritizing. Ideas that have little support from the majority of the members should at this point be discarded. Some features of the community may be strengths, but they may also have very limited tourist appeal. Therefore, they could not be the focus of a successful marketing strategy. For example, the committee may list a single exhibit on the area's history at the local museum or the existence of a local group that performs operatic music, as strengths on which an event might be based. Both of these are strengths in which the community can take pride, but they are not strong enough attractions on their own to develop and promote as an event as the external analysis did not demonstrate that there is a large enough interest. After the strengths with limited appeal are deleted from the list, what will remain are the major strengths that can be used to develop an event. If there are several, the committee then must prioritize by choosing the most feasible.

After consensus is reached on an event idea, the same process of listing and prioritizing is repeated for the weaknesses that can prove to be threats. The prioritizing is particularly important, as the organization has limited resources that can be used to correct weaknesses. Therefore, the weaknesses that the group prioritizes as critical should be those that are most likely to detract from the possible success of an event. For example, one of the community's strengths may be that there are many historic buildings in its downtown area. However, if a weakness is the poor condition of the storefronts and streets, this must be corrected before an event involving tours of the historic buildings can be developed. If the internal analysis shows that funding is limited and restoration is not possible, then this idea should be discarded. Another example of a critical weakness is if the community lacks the necessary supporting products of adequate lodging and food establishments. The committee must then work with local business people or the local economic development authority to encourage the expansion of these services.

After compiling lists of major strengths and critical weaknesses, the committees will next focus on opportunities and threats. Community members have a vital role to play during the first two steps in the SWOT analysis process of determining strengths and weakness as they have an intimate knowledge of what the community has to offer. However, local citizens may not have as much knowledge of external opportunities and threats. While everyone should be involved in suggesting opportunities and threats that will be listed and prioritized, the final decision on what opportunities will be the focus of the event will be the responsibility of tourism officials. The type of event is a strategic decision that must be based on the availability of resources and the possibility of success. However it is still important to have everyone on the committee involved in the analysis process to help build consensus.

Discussion questions

- Why it is necessary to ensure government and community support the planned event?
- What role do civic groups and local businesses play in ensuring the success of an event?
- What types of event decisions would be affected by the economic, socio-cultural and technological forces in the external environment?
- How does the organization mission and values statement affect the attendance decision?
- Why should external threats and opportunities be analyzed?
- How do the internal strengths and weaknesses help determine the plan?
- How are objectives and tasks determined?

Case

Don't forget the locals

While you are hoping to attract visitors to your event the community might be hoping not so many visitors arrive. Why? The community may be concerned that the visitors will bring traffic congestion, noise, crowding and even possible crime. One way to build community support for your tourism event is to hold a small pre-event just for community members. The event is to gather community members for enjoyment but also to provide an opportunity for you to explain the purpose of the event and the benefits it will provide. Of course, you could have a community meeting but who will want to attend? Here are some easy, inexpensive and fun ideas for gathering the community at an event rather than just a meeting.

- Street party: Close off a street by the venue, provide the pizza or other inexpensive food and watch people show up.
- Street or wall art: Get out the chalk and let the community help decorate the event site. This brings authenticity to a new level.
- Talent show: Use the event stage to host a local talent show the night before the event opens. The winner gets to perform at the event!
- Bonfire: If you are having your event outdoors, use the venue site to have a traditional bonfire. People have always loved to gather around warmth.
- Swap Shop: Select a theme such as children's toys. Then have people bring the ones their kids have outgrown to swap for ones that will be new to their kids (Starchild 2019).

Task: What event idea could be used to build community support?

Case

Social media and scanning the external environment

All organizations now understand they need to include social media in their marketing strategies. However many still do not understand that social media can be used to conduct research on their customers, competitors and trends. The information that is discovered can be useful in many ways.

- Remain customer-centric: When social listening results in discovering customer complaints, the company can respond immediately by addressing the issue within the organization or improving the product.
- Learn trends: Trends are continually changing, so marketing strategy needs to continually evolve to take advantage of these changes.
- Understand pain points: Listening to customer complaints about competing products can provide information for future improvements.
- Develop marketing strategy: Simply finding out where consumers are having product discussions will let companies know on what social media sites they should have a presence.
- Discover competitive advantage: The company may discover from positive comments made on review sites a new product benefit of which they were unaware (Nair 2019).

Task: What kinds of information can social media provide on both your visitors and visitors to competing events?

Event plan: Use the information from this chapter to complete the first section of the event plan outline at the end of the book.

References

Ahmed, Wasim. 2019. "Using Twitter as a Data Source: An Overview of Social Media Research Tools (2019)." *London School of Economics Blog.* June 18, 2019. https://blogs.lse.ac.uk/impactofsocialsciences/2019/06/18/using-twitter-as-a-data-source-an-overview-of-social-media-research-tools-2019/. Accessed September 19, 2020.

Brandenburger, Adam. 2019. "Are Your Company's Strengths Really Weaknesses?" *Harvard Business Review.* August 22, 2019. https://hbr.org/2019/08/are-your-companys-strengths-really-weaknesses. Accessed February 22, 2019.

Chrisos, Marianne. 2019. "What Is the Negative Impact of Mobile Technology on Business Communication". *Tech Funnel.* May 16, 2019. https://www.techfunnel.com/information-technology/what-is-the-negative-impact-of-mobile-tech-on-business-communications/. Accessed December 12, 2019.

Constantin, Marguax, Steve Saxon, and Jackey Yu. 2020. "Reimagining the 9 Trillion Tourism Economy – What Will it Take?" August 15, 2020. https://www.mckinsey.com/

industries/travel-logistics-and-transport-infrastructure/our-insights/reimagining-the-9-tr
illion-tourism-economy-what-will-it-take#. Accessed November 1, 2020.

Ferrell, O.C., Dana E. Harrison, Linda Ferrell, and Joe F. Hair. 2019. "Business Ethics, Corporate Social Responsibility and Brand Attitudes: An Exploratory Study." *Journal of Business Research* 95, 491–501.

Fresch, Marino. 2019. "SMART Goals for Event Planners." *Eventbrite Blog UK*. June 3, 2019. https://www.eventbrite.co.uk/blog/goal-setting-for-event-planners-ds00/. Accessed October 26, 2020.

Glassman, Jim. 2019. "Will Consumers Stop Spending?" *JP Morgan*. January 30, 2019. https://www.jpmorgan.com/commercial-banking/insights/will-consumers-stop-spending. Accessed November 14, 2020.

Gorny, Nina. 2018. "SWOT Analysis - A Useful Tool for Event Planners." *Konfeo*. June 4, 2018. https://www.konfeo.com/en/blog/swot-analysis-a-useful-tool-for-event-planners/. Accessed September 17, 2020.

Nair, Ranjit. 2019. "Five Reasons Small Organizations Should Invest in Social Listening." *Entrepreneur*. April 15, 2019. https://www.entrepreneur.com/article/331791. Accessed August 17, 2020.

Pawinska Sims, Maja. 2018. "Study: Higher Consumer Expectations Push Brands to Deliver on Innovation Ethics and Functionality". September 12, 2018. https://www.holmesreport.com/latest/article/study-higher-consumer-expectations-push-brands-to-deliver-on-innovation-ethics-and-functionality. Accessed August 30, 2019.

Roy, Riyanka. 2019. "How Social Networks Can Contribute Towards Responsible Tourism." *Thrive Global*. July 4, 2019. https://thriveglobal.com/stories/how-social-networks-can-contribute-towards-responsible-tourism/. Accessed October 31, 2020.

Starchild, Zara. 2019. "10 Community Event Ideas to Bring Everyone Together." *EventBright Blog*. June 24, 2019. https://www.eventbrite.co.uk/blog/community-event-ideas-ds00/. Accessed September 2, 2020.

Stavans, I. and J. Ellison. 2015. *Reclaiming Travel*. Durham, NC: Duke University Press.

Chapter 4

Targeting the event visitor segment

Abstract

The decision to attend an event is not always a simple process. Some products are inexpensive and purchased routinely with little thought put into the purchase. Products that are more expensive and less frequently bought will require the purchaser to research competitors. Extensive research and thought will go into expensive and difficult-to-understand products. Social media has changed the research process as consumers become aware of travel opportunities when they view postings about trips from other travelers. Organizations with limited marketing capacity may decide to focus their promotion on a single visitor segment. To target multiple segments requires an event that can meet the desires of more than one group. Positioning an event means ensuring that unique benefits are communicated to the targeted segment. Visitors are grouped into segments based on common characteristics and desires. One or more segments may be targeted. The visitors can be segmented by geographic location. The goal might be to target only local residents, or those in the region or from an even wider geographic area. Visitors can be grouped based on demographic characteristics such as age, income, gender or ethnicity. Most widely used is psychographic segmentation that groups visitors on values, attitudes and lifestyle.

Event attendance decision-making process

Consumers may not always consider the process they go through when deciding why or how to purchase a product, take a trip or attend an event. However, marketers must understand the process so that the correct promotional message can be provided at the appropriate time. Products can be categorized by the three methods used when purchasing. The promotional message and how it is communicated will differ depending on whether the product purchase process is routine, involves limited research or involves extensive research.

Routine purchase decisions

Some products are purchased routinely without much thought. These are products, such as soap, that are inexpensive and widely available. In travel, a routine purchase would be an inexpensive car rental. As long as the car will get the visitor from place to place, not much consideration is given to such features as brand or color. Most visitors will not be willing to research rental car companies to find a specific car color. If a wrong purchase decision is made when making a routine purchase, the consequences are not serious. An unattractive color of a rental car will be ignored if the price is attractive. If the color of a rental car is not the visitor's favorite one, the car will still provide the needed benefit of transportation.

Now even products that are purchased routinely are being enhanced so that the purchaser is willing to pay more. Even routine travel products can now be marketed as a specialty product that needs to be researched (Watamanuk 2018). For example, car rentals can now be marketed offering the traveler the opportunity to drive a car they could never afford to buy or to make an environmentally correct choice by renting an electric vehicle. This trend has been reinforced by the use of Instagram sites and influencer recommendations. Social media can now be used by travel organizations to show that a formerly routine product such as an event t-shirt is now specialized by using handcrafted techniques or natural fibers, to reach a segment of visitors that are willing to pay more to bring home a unique souvenir of their trip.

Limited involvement purchase decisions

Products that are more expensive and complex require limited involvement resulting in the consumer spending more time making the purchase decision. Most events fall into this category. The visitor must spend their resources of money and time when attending so they want to only go to events that provide benefits they will enjoy. They may have multiple choices on what events they can attend and will research online both the information provided by the organization and other past attender recommendations. To help them make an informed attendance decision, the organization must provide information on the event's unique features and the benefits attendance will provide.

With this type of product purchase, the potential visitor has familiarity with all the many types of events that they might attend. To encourage the decision to attend their event, the organization must explain their event's competitive advantage. For example, if potential visitors are looking for a music festival, they already know that there are many different types that they can attend. They need to be able to find the information online on who is performing, what other activities will be available and why the purchase price is appropriate. This decision to attend can also be heavily influenced by recommendations by past visitors. Since marketing communications are not trusted, the organization must ensure that potential visitors see the recommendations and photos that are online by linking them to their own social media and website.

Extensive involvement consumer decisions

Purchases that require extensive involvement are high-priced and complex. If someone is considering attending an event that is at a distance and lasts several days, they will do more research. Because the risk of making a wrong decision will be financially costly and also use limited holiday time, more time and research will be needed before the attendance decision is finally made. To influence the purchase decision, the marketer must not only provide information but use sales techniques to motivate the potential visitor to make the attendance decision.

Again, technology has changed this process. The potential visitor will expect to be able to use technology such as a chatbot to get immediate responses to requests for information. They may also tweet their questions about the event. The organization needs to respond with enough information so that the potential visitor is comfortable buying tickets to even expensive multi-day events requiring extensive research.

Types of decision-making

- Routine: Bought frequently without much thought.
- Limited: Because of cost and choices, more time for research.
- Extensive: Expensive and complex products need much research.

Consumer buying process

The steps in the purchase process for consumers has been described as consisting of the steps of need recognition, search for information, evaluation of alternatives, purchase and post-purchase assessment. While this model is still useful for many products, because of the use of social media the decision to attend an event often follows a different path. Rather than the process starting with recognizing the need to travel, the desire to travel is motivated when searching for other types of information. Consumers may be looking at social media when a photo or video of an event catches their attention. This then triggers a desire for travel which wasn't present before the information was seen. The potential visitor has already found an event online. Now they need help in determining if this is the right travel decision (Harrison 2019). Rather than starting with an awareness that they need to attend an event, the process starts when a potential visitor encounters information online about an upcoming event of which they were previously unaware. As a result, a new purchase process model that incorporated social media use has been developed consisting of three steps of awareness, consideration and purchase.

In a traditional marketing model, the first step is the consumer seeking out information to meet a need or solve a problem. As a result, traditional tourism promotion started with advertising to communicate the fact that a location existed to fill the need for a holiday. However, now it is more likely that a consumer will come across a travel location or event through casual online browsing while doing an online search or through the use of social media. As a result, they will first discover the event and then realize they want to attend. Therefore, the tourism and hospitality marketer must use not only their own website but also social media, including blog posts, and post photos and videos on other sites to ensure awareness of their event.

Once the potential visitor is aware of the event, the consideration stage involves the consumer searching for more information. Marketers must understand that there is an abundance of already existing, easily assessable, information about events online. However, marketers can still influence consideration by using promotion to direct potential visitors to their own website where customer reviews, photos, videos and detailed information can be provided. It is essential that the organization has their voice heard during the consideration process. If they are silent, the potential visitor will believe any negative comments that they find online are true. Therefore, the organization must ensure that their positive message is communicated using as many social media sites as possible.

The final step in the process is purchase of the product. Potential visitors may take considerable time during the consideration process reading reviews and looking at social media sites. However, when they finally decide to attend, they want to finish the purchase process immediately. For this reason, the process of ticket purchase and hotel reservations has to be as convenient as possible. Packaging all event components into one easy purchase can help the process.

Social media and event attendance process

The use of social media has changed every step of how consumers purchase products, including tourism (TripAdvisor 2018). During the first step of awareness, the inspiration for travel is rarely based on information from a travel intermediary. Instead, someone might be online updating their Facebook page or perusing information on a video or photo-sharing site when they notice that someone has posted information on their experience at an event. This might prompt a desire to also attend a specific event. The decision was not motivated by any promotional material produced by the tourism organization. The consideration stage has also been affected by social media. Rather than request information from the organization, the potential visitor is much more likely to then search social networking sites to find information posted by other visitors. As a result, the organization marketing the event is only one of many sources of information that influence the attendance decision.

Once the decision has been made to attend, it used to be thought that the search for information was completed. However social media has also changed this step in the consumer behavior process as visitors continue to search for information even while the event is taking place. The visitor is using social media to continually customize their visit experience, by seeing what other people are experiencing at the event and destination.

Another change resulting from social media is that the evaluation of the event experience now starts during the event not after (Carnoy 2018). While in the past a common motivation ascribed to travel was a desire to get away from everyday life, now the visitor stays in contact with home while away. In the past, the traveler had to wait until they arrived home to share their trip photos. Now visitors start sharing while on the trip via social media. They do so as part of the event experience. While social media is used to enrich the trip by sharing information with those back home, visitors also use it to communicate with local residents to find unique experiences.

After the trip, social media is used to critique the trip by writing reviews and sharing the trip by posting photos. While it may have been the technologically sophisticated trendsetters who first used online sites to directly access tourism products and social media to share experiences, this change in consumer behavior spread rapidly until it is now the accepted means of purchasing any travel experience.

Visitor segmentation strategy

Before the organization decides what visitor segments to target with promotional information on their event, they must decide how many different segments of potential visitors can be motivated to attend. For this reason, it is necessary to decide if an undifferentiated, concentrated or multisegmented strategy is appropriate. An undifferentiated strategy assumes everyone will be equally motivated to attend and targets everyone with the same promotional message. A concentrated strategy is the opposite, where only a single segment of visitors who it is believed will most likely be interested in attendance is targeted with promotion. A multisegmented strategy targets more than one segment, with a different promotional message designed for each.

Undifferentiated segmentation

It might be tempting to try to maximize attendance by targeting all potential visitors. This is done in the belief that visitors are an undifferentiated mass of people who all desire the same benefits from attendance at an event. This may have worked in the past when there were fewer events and people did not travel frequently. The local fair or festival could count on attendance from community members and visitors because there were not many opportunities for relaxation and socialization. Now people have many options for attending events and the time and money to do so. Because of social media they are also now aware of the many varied benefits that different events provide. Unless the event promotion speaks directly to the targeted visitor segment with a specific message as to the benefit provided, it will be ignored. While all events offer the opportunity for socialization and activities, different events will promote their distinct advantage whether for family fun, best event for pets, or where to interact with others with the same interests.

Concentrated segmentation

An event that is promoted as meeting the needs of every potential visitor will not motivate attendance. Even with a product as simple as soap, product variations have been developed to attract specific customers. There is now designer branded soap, environmentally correct soap, soap for sensitive skin and soap for particularly dirty people. The common marketing practice today is to segment the market into segments of consumers based on similar product needs and desires. The organization then targets a promotional message at the group who are most likely to desire their product.

A concentrated targeting strategy for an event is one where a single group of potential visitors is targeted. The event is designed with this group in mind when considering what type of activities and other supporting products to include. A promotional message is then designed to communicate these benefits. The message is then posted on the media that is most likely to reach this segment. For a small tourism organization or single hotel hosting an event, a concentrated strategy is often chosen because only one promotional campaign needs to be developed. If the event grows in popularity, they may then decide to target an additional visitor segment with new benefits and a unique promotional message.

Multisegmented segmentation

A multisegmented targeting strategy is used when more than one group of potential visitors is targeted. For example, a garden festival might target both families with young children and older adults. Even if both groups want to attend an event about gardens, the price and activities desired may differ. The families might be offered a discounted price that includes all members. The families might want educational activities that involve active participation, while older adults may not be offered a discount as price does not affect their ability to attend. The older adult garden lovers might be interested in educational seminars about the history of garden design. As a result, a unique marketing message must be created for each segment. Small organizations will most likely have a concentrated targeting strategy as it takes resources to target more than one group. As an event grows in popularity and size it may target more segments. While targeting more than one segment requires additional time and money, it can also increase revenue by attracting new visitor segments.

Segmentation strategies

- Undifferentiated: Treating all consumers as having the same product needs.
- Concentrated: Choosing one segment that will desire product benefits.
- Multi-segmented: Choosing more than one segment each with unique needs.

Determining the visitor segment to target

The easiest method of segmenting visitors is to use demographic and geographic characteristics. Using available data such as a government census, organizations can determine the age, gender and family status characteristics of a population. Using the same data, they can easily determine where potential visitors live. They can then create and communicate promotional messages to target a specific consumer segment.

While these methods of segmentation are still in use, it is now more common to segment consumers based on psychographic characteristics such as values, attitudes and lifestyles (Rogers 2019). In the past, it was difficult to determine who shared these internal variables. Now, people form communities online based on these traits. Organizations can then analyze which of these groups would find messages about their event of interest.

Segmentation can be based on any characteristic such as family status or interest in a specific art form. However, whatever basis is chosen, the resulting group of individuals targeted must be large enough to make the time and money spent doing so worthwhile. For example, a segment of people over age 70 living in a small town attending an accordion festival will not provide enough revenue for the event to be successful.

Self-segmentation on social media

The segmentation of consumers into groups is based on the fact that shared characteristics result in shared product needs and desires has been established marketing theory. Segmentation was developed because sending out promotional messages uses the resources of time, talent and money. As it is known that consumers differ as to the product benefits they desire, it makes sense to save resources by sending promotional messages to only the group of consumers most likely to purchase. However, the rise of social media has meant that tourism and hospitality marketers must be cautious in over-relying on segmentation.

Today consumers depend less on promotional messages for product information and more on receiving information about products through their social networks. Interest in the product then spreads via social media. As a result, the organization is in danger of ignoring groups of consumers that were not targeted but rather found the product through word-of-mouth online. While it is still appropriate to segment and target groups of consumers most likely to purchase, organizations must always be analyzing social media to determine if interest is being evidenced by a new group that was not targeted. They can do so by monitoring social media sites to see what type of people are expressing an interest in attending. The organization can then make the choice whether it is worthwhile to further develop this organically grown segment.

Geographic segmentation

One of the decisions that an organization must make is on the geographic scope of their promotion efforts. Targeting too large a geographic area to promote attendance is challenging. Visitors may not wish to travel a long distance for a small event. However, this same segment may be willing to travel an even longer distance for a well-known event. Of course, there are no geographic restrictions for social media marketing, but other traditional forms of motivation will need to be duplicated in each geographic area that is targeted. For this reason the geographic boundaries of the visitor segment must be determined.

The decision to target a city or region to attract visitors must consider both the size of the geographic region and also the population density. If the urban population targeted is in a small geographic area, it is possible that there will still be enough potential customers. If the potential visitors live in rural communities that have a more dispersed population, a larger geographic area is needed to ensure adequate attendance. Geographic segmentation does not mean that the organization is uninterested in attracting visitors from other areas; it only means that promotion will be concentrated on the chosen locations.

Since local residents are already nearby it seems easy to add them as a geographic segment. There still needs to be further segmentation as to what group of local residents are being targeted (Voges 2020). If local couples are targeted, a separate marketing message communicating that the event is a perfect "date night" opportunity could be used. There may also need to be discounts to attract local families, if that is the targeted segment.

Demographic segmentation

Of course, using geographic location alone as a base for segmentation is insufficient. Many people with different attendance and travel preferences will live in the same area. Therefore, the next step is to consider demographic segmentation. Some of the most common demographic descriptors that are used when segmenting include age, family life cycle, gender and ethnic background. For example, age is used when considering who will be potential visitors as some events are specifically designed for a single age group, such as a flower festival for older visitors and an electronic music concert for younger ones. However, even these generalities are often blurred as young people like gardens and older people enjoy reliving their youth through music.

Age is used as a predictor of product preference because in a rapidly changing world, different age groups have had different life experiences. For example, young people who have grown up with technology will expect it to be integrated into as many experiences as possible. Older people also use technology but may not consider it necessary for an enjoyable experience. Age alone cannot be used as a descriptor because with older people living longer healthier lives, they may now prefer experiences such as sports festivals that this age group may not have preferred in the past.

A better method of approaching demographic segmentation is to think of the family life cycle, which affects both spending potential and the events attended. This cycle tends to occur for most people but will do so at varying ages. Young people typically are just starting out in careers and, therefore, have limited income. As a result they will be looking for nearby, inexpensive experiences. As they age they will have better-paying jobs, but without a partner or children. At this stage they will have income to spend and be interested in travel and other leisure activities that provide an upscale experience. With a partner, children or both they will be interested in event experiences that meet the educational needs of their children. Once this stage of life is finished and the children are grown, they will again have money to spend on attending events with benefits they desire.

Another demographic descriptor is gender. While some products are still used only by men or women, this is rarely true of event experiences. Even though both genders may be interested in attendance, different benefits may appeal to each gender. In this case, separate promotional messages may be developed. Because of social changes, event experiences that were formerly seen to be desired by one gender, such as cooking events for women and auto shows for men, are now desired by both (O'Reilly 2019). The promotional message then needs to be changed so that it features words and images meant to appeal to both genders. However, events that are promoted to both genders may still require separate promotional messages for each if the desired benefits differ.

Another descriptor of demographic segmentation is ethnicity. This can be challenging to use when segmenting visitors as it can be seen as stereotyping. However, the targeting is based on the fact that ethnic groups may share certain values resulting in similar patterns of living. The consumption choices for types of entertainment, travel and lodging may result from their cultural backgrounds. This is true even when members of a minority group have integrated into the majority culture (Webber 2017). For example, certain holidays may be celebrated by an ethnic group. The celebration may be a possible focus for a tourism event. It is then appropriate to target this group with a promotional message. The promotional message will need to be delivered using the social and other media that is mostly commonly seen by members of the ethnic group.

Ethnic segmentation can also take into account other behavior patterns. Some ethnic groups stress the importance of the extended family group. If the event being promoted is entertainment, then the benefits provided by a performance targeted at this ethnic group would stress that it can be enjoyed by a wide range of ages. Ethnic pride can also be used as an appealing product attribute. The fact that the event is focused on a particular country or the performer shares an ethnic background can be used to target a specific ethnic group.

Importance of psychographic visitor characteristics

Psychographic segmentation based on values, attitudes and lifestyles is probably the most useful tool for organizations promoting events. Some products, such as food, clothing and shelter, are needed in order for people to survive, but attendance at events fills other desires. This is particularly true for event experiences that are purchased because of visitors' values, attitudes and lifestyles.

Psychographic characteristics can vary widely. For example, visitors who value fun will wish to participate in entertaining activities at events. Other visitors who value education will attend events that have activities from which they can learn. Social media now can be used to provide information on visitors' psychographic characteristics (Graves and Matz 2018). By analyzing social media usage, such as what sites are visited and what topics are liked, the organization can design tailored messages based on potential visitors' values, attitudes and lifestyles. Although using psychographic characteristics makes determining the potential size of the market more difficult, research using social media sources can help find the answer. For example, if postings on a social media site express the desire for events that involve physical activity for the entire family, this is an indicator that there will be sufficient potential visitors for a sports festival. However, this psychographic information must be combined with geographic characteristics of where the segment lives and also with demographic characteristics such as age and family status.

Values, which are deeply held beliefs of how life should be lived, are learned from family members as well as from outside organizations such as school, religion and social clubs. Values usually remain the same for a lifetime. Visitors may decide to attend an event in a geographic location because they share the values of that community. For example, while visitors are able to attend many events, they may decide to attend an event that stresses environmental sustainability because visitors feel they can enjoy themselves without guilt. Marketers must not only communicate the benefit of the event, but also communicate the values of the community or organization staging the event to the targeted visitor segment.

While it would be difficult to change the values of a visitor, their attitude, which is a preconceived idea about an event, can be changed. For example, visitors might have the attitude that attending music festivals is only for the young. This attitude might have been formed from seeing social media postings targeted at this group. Therefore, a promotional message would be needed to show visuals of older people interacting with musicians and enjoying the event. Of course, not all older visitors will become interested, but some attitudes will be changed.

Lifestyle groups, people who associate voluntarily because they share an interest, affect how people will spend their time. Young people will often choose a group whose lifestyle will differentiate them from their parents and other family members. An example of a lifestyle group is one that follows a particular sports team. Other lifestyle groups may form around popular culture trends such as using the latest technology. Culture and creative interests also support lifestyle groups. An online group may form on the basis of enjoying a particular cultural product, such as opera. They may also form around those who wish to participate in creativity even if their talent is limited, for example, a group that works in fiber arts. By promoting to such lifestyle groups, organizers can create an event that provides access to information and proximity to others who share that interest. In return, these community members will not only be excited about attending the event, they will also promote the event to others in their group using personal contact and social media.

Segmentation characteristics with examples

- Demographic: Age, family status, income, ethnicity.
- Geographic: Local, regional, urban, rural.

- Psychographic lifestyle: Athletic, adventurous, thrift shoppers, foodies, travelers.
- Psychographic attitudes: Fun-loving, serene, traditional, family-focused.
- Psychographic values: Spiritual, nature, fashionistas, spiritual.

Positioning the event

By now the organization has determined the event benefits and decided upon the visitor segment they will target based on geographic, demographic and psychographic characteristics. In addition, they have decided to target either a single segment or more than one segment. Now that the organization knows to which segment of potential visitors the event's benefits will be communicated, it might seem that the process is finished. However, there is one more issue, product positioning, that needs to be considered.

No event or travel experience is alone in the marketplace. Instead, it is grouped in the visitor's mind with competing events, all of which are promoted as having similar experience benefits, such as family-friendly or trend setting. Positioning the event, the final step in the segmentation process, is when the organization considers how to communicate to the potential visitor the difference between the benefits offered by their event and those offered by competitors. The event can be positioned positively against competitors. For example, an organization might promote that their event supports local musicians in a way that attending a festival showcasing a well-known entertainer does not. Instead of taking the positive route, the organization may position the competing event negatively. The marketing message might include the fact that the competing event is harmful to both the environment and the local economy.

Product positioning can be based on a number of factors. The event can be positioned based on overall attributes such as price or quality. For example, the event might be positioned as being the lowest priced among competing events. If the event cannot compete on price, the organization may position the event against the competition as having higher quality. Or the event may be positioned based on specific features that other events lack, such as being the only event of the year that is showing a specific type of entertainment.

In addition, positioning can also be based on the status of the event's brand image. For example, the organization may decide to position attendance as having a status that attending other events does not offer. This is particularly true because event attributes can be difficult to compare. For example, attending the first night of an event does not guarantee a better experience. In fact, the opposite may be true as there may yet be details to work out. Instead, attending the first night of the event is positioned as a status symbol. More visitors will attend the event at a later date, but only a select few are able to attend the first night.

Positioning may not stay stable over time. Sometimes the original positioning strategy must be changed to accommodate changing travel trends. In this case it is said that the product is repositioned. An example might be a product that was originally positioned as family-friendly. However, if, over time, many other family-friendly events are launched in the area, then the event may be repositioned as having a unique feature such as activities for young adults.

Discussion questions

1. How do consumers make purchase decisions?
2. Why don't consumers use the routine purchase decision process while buying expensive products?
3. Why should the undifferentiated segmentation strategy be avoided?
4. When is a multi-segment strategy appropriate?
5. Why should potential visitors be segmented by common characteristics?
6. Why shouldn't a segmentation strategy only focus on demographic characteristics?
7. What type of psychographic characteristics could be used to segment visitors?

Case

What do seekers of authenticity really want?

There is a significant segment of potential visitors who want an authentic experience when they travel. This is particularly true of younger visitors. They want convenience but they also say they don't want a prepackaged experience that is devoid of influences from the surrounding community. They don't see holidays as a way just to escape from reality in order to have fun. They want to have fun but while experiencing a new and different reality. What they are looking for can be summarized as the following.

- Stay active: Maybe because they are younger, they want experiences that involve physical activity rather than being a passive observer. A physical activity allows them to interact with the landscape, not just view it.
- Self-discovery: While wanting to learn about a different culture, such travelers equally want to learn about themselves. They expect to come away from the travel experience changed in some way. They want to go home with an idea for anything from a new hobby to a new way of living.
- Be unique: They don't want to go to well-known destinations where everyone else is going. They want to travel to a new destination that is smaller and off the tourist path. While there they want to take local transportation and shop at the local markets.
- Share online: Once they have had their unique and active journey of self-discovery, they want to share it with the rest of the world. This increases visits to the formerly lesser-known site by other visitors. Seekers of authentic experiences will then need to find another place to visit (Mya 2020).

Task: How can your event meet the needs of this segment of potential visitors?

Case

There are advantages to virtual events

There was always the choice to hold events virtually, but such events were rare. The pandemic of 2020 took away the choice. If the event wasn't held virtually it couldn't be held at all. While in-person events have the advantage of travel to a pleasant location and the opportunity to network while at the same time learning, virtual events also have advantages for attendees. Here are some that can be promoted the next time you are planning a virtual event.

- You don't have to worry about it being cancelled due to weather, union strikes or other unforeseen events.
- Costs for rental and setup are eliminated, which means that the registration cost can be less.
- By having lower attendance fees, groups who would have been excluded because of the cost can now attend and have their voices heard.
- Attendees no longer have the cost of travel and hotel rooms, which were a barrier to attendance.
- Virtual events have less negative effective on the environment.
- Sessions are recorded so that attendees will never miss a session because of jet lag or double booking.
- Networking for introverts is easier because they don't have to face a crowded ballroom where everyone is listening to the extroverts.

Virtual events are not better or worse than in-person events. They are just different (Team GTR 2020)!

Task: How can some activity at your event become virtual if it needs to be?

Event plan: Use the information from this chapter to complete the first section of the event plan outline at the end of the book.

References

Carnoy, Juliet. 2018. "5 Ways Social Media Has Transformed Tourism Marketing." *Entrepreneur.* March 12, 2018. https://www.entrepreneur.com/article/286408. Accessed November 16, 2020.

Graves, Christopher and Sandra Matz. 2018. "What Marketers Should Know about Personality Based Marketing." *Harvard Business Review.* May 21, 2018. https://hbr.org/2018/05/what-marketers-should-know-about-personality-based-marketing. Accessed March 20, 2020.

Harrison, Kate. 2019. "Decoding How Customers Buy (and Why They Don't)." *Forbes.* February 27, 2019. https://www.forbes.com/sites/kateharrison/2019/02/27/decoding-how-customers-buy-and-why-they-dont/?sh=fdfb3c9330fe. Accessed September 24, 2020.

May, Kace. 2020. "Why Millennial Travelers Are Seeking More Authentic Experiences." *Under 30 Experiences.* October 5, 2020. https://www.under30experiences.com/blog/why-millenial-travelers-are-seeking-more-authentic-experiences. Accessed October 23, 2020.

O'Reilly, Lara. 2019. "Some Marketers Moving Away from Dated Gender Targeting, Study Shows." *Wall Street Journal*. January 28, 2019. https://www.wsj.com/articles/some-marketers-moving-away-from-dated-gender-targeting-study-shows-11548673201. Accessed December 12, 2020.

Rogers, Charlotte. 2019. "Why Behavior Beats Demographics When It Comes to Segmentation." *Marketing Week*. April 16, 2019. https://www.marketingweek.com/behaviour-demographics-segmentation/. Accessed November 2, 2020.

Team GTR. 2020. "10 Benefits of Virtual Events." *GTR Now*. July 27, 2020. https://gtrnow.com/10-benefits-of-virtual-events/. Accessed April 1, 2020.

TripAdvisor. 2018. "An Overview of the Traveler Path to Purchase." *TripAdvisor*. March 12, 2018. https://www.tripadvisor.com/TripAdvisorInsights/w2532. Accessed November 3, 2010.

Voges, Lauren. 2020. "10 Ways to Attract Locals to Your Museum or Attraction." *Tiqets*. August 27, 2020. https://www.tiqets.com/venues/blog/attract-tourists/. Accessed November 2, 2020.

Watamanuk, Tyler. 2018. "When Did Soap, Once Simple, Get so Complicated?" *New York Times*. July 7, 2018. https://www.nytimes.com/2018/07/11/style/whats-the-best-soap.html. Accessed July 17, 2020.

Webber, Richard. 2017. "Why It's Not Racist for Marketers to Treat Ethnic Groups Differently." *Global Market Alliance*. July 5, 2017. https://www.the-gma.com/marketers-ethnic-groups. Accessed January 3, 2020.

Chapter 5

Researching potential visitors

Abstract

Research needs to be conducted to understand what event benefits will attract visitors. Research can also answer questions about an acceptable price, preferred venue and promotional message for the event. Research is a process that starts with a question and results in recommendations. If the correct research question is not asked, the results will not be of use. Descriptive quantitative research answers questions of what, when and who. Exploratory qualitative research answers the more important question of why visitors attend events. Because not everyone can be asked to participate in research, sampling is used. While there are online tools for writing descriptive surveys, time must still be spent on writing the questions and answers so the right information is obtained. Links to surveys can now be attached to social media postings. Exploratory research is used to understand visitor motivation. Focus groups where potential visitors are asked open-ended questions allow them to answer in their own words. Interviews do take time but can result in a deeper understanding of motivation or problems.

Researching desired visitor benefits

The tourism, hospitality and event management industries are interrelated because the same consumer will most likely desire services from all three industries. Some visitors are coming for a specific event but will also need food from restaurants, food markets or takeouts. If the trip is longer than a day, they will need lodging at a service hotel, a less expensive motel or in a private home. While at the location for the event they are attending, these same individuals will need other activities to occupy their time.

The types of events that are produced by organizations to attract visitors are varied and include music, theatre, festivals, carnivals and parades. Before, during and after an event there is a need to conduct research of their current and potential visitors to determine how each of these events can best meet their needs. This is true of even the largest tourist attractions that continually research visitor preferences before, during and after the visit (Kaemingk 2018). To do so they have staff interview guests, send email surveys and also solicit feedback on apps.

Secondary data

Providing an unforgettable experience for travelers is still at the heart of the tourism, hospitality and event management industries. As a result, while the products they offer will differ, all three industries share a similar need to conduct consumer research to understand changing visitor expectations.

Before conducting research these organizations might be able to find existing information that is already available online or in print. This type of information is referred to as secondary data. It is available from databases that include information provided by government sources, academic studies or trade organization research. With the growth of the use of social media there are now new sources of secondary information. This is such a new phenomenon that the method of analyzing this type of data is still being developed (Beaulac 2019). However, in the meantime, insights can still be gained by examining these secondary social media sources.

Researching the visitor experience

The purpose of research is to provide the information the organization needs to determine the correct product, price, place and promotion that will motivate the potential visitor. They gather this information by researching both facts about visitors and also their opinions and preferences. The research can focus on improving the event product, learning the correct price, determining the appropriate venue location and learning the best method for promotional communication

The organization needs to research potential visitors to learn if their planned event will provide the benefits that will motivate attendance. It isn't enough to just know that visitors want entertainment. The research needs to understand what type of entertainment will motivate potential visitors to attend an event. In addition, potential visitors must be researched to learn what type of lodging they desire. This is because people want more from lodging than just a place to spend the night. The research should focus on what other desires are important to visitors, such as safety, cleanliness, relaxation or socialization. The hotel should not assume it knows the answer but instead conduct research on an ongoing basis of potential and current guests to obtain this information. If the organization is going to offer an event with the benefits visitors desire they must know as much as possible about their current and potential visitors. This would include researching demographic data such as gender, age, income and education level. It would also include researching psychographic information such as their values, attitudes and lifestyles.

Setting prices is one of the most complex issues facing an organization. They need to charge enough to cover expenses and make a profit. At the same they must try to keep their prices low as they know potential visitors are comparing prices online. The purpose of pricing research is to determine the correct price that will encourage attendance. Research can also discover if there are added services and experiences for which visitors are willing to pay. Place or distribution refers to the physical location where the event is held. Visitors understand that the location is related to price as more upscale locations, such as near an ocean with a view, will cost more. The question that needs to be researched is how much more they will be willing to pay. Location research can also deal with convenience as visitors may be concerned about saving time and be willing to pay more to attend an event that does not require expensive transportation. Only research will determine if the location is acceptable.

Promotion may be the marketing component that is most frequently researched. A good deal of money and time is spent on designing promotional material in the hope that it will effectively communicate a compelling marketing message. Using research to determine what marketing message will motivate attendance and how it should be communicated means that there can be less reliance on hope and more reliance on fact regarding what words and images will motivate a visit.

Research topics

- Visitors: Benefits desired, demographic and psychographic facts.
- Pricing: Appropriate price level.
- Place: Type and location of venue.
- Promotion: Message and media.

Research process

To conduct effective marketing research, an organization needs to understand the entire research process. Understanding the process will help the tourism and hospitality organizations plan their research so their efforts will be successful in providing the needed information. Without planning, either the organization will not obtain enough information to justify the research cost and effort or they will obtain information, but not what is needed.

The research process can be summarized as the need to decide what to ask, whom to ask and how to ask. The first step involves the organization in determining what information is needed, which will require writing the research question. For example, a tourism organization may need to know what would attract visitors to events during the off season. While this might seem an appropriate question, it is too broad. The question needs to be narrowed to a specific type of visitor that will be the subject of the research. It might also need to be narrowed by activity. For example, a hospitality management company may want to know what type of activities couples prefer during the winter months.

Next, the organization must decide where this information can be obtained. If the research question is general to the population, such as how many people attended music festivals last year, the data is probably already available. For example, a music trade association has the means to conduct this type of research and will already have this information. If the research question is what type of music local people prefer, then the organization will need to conduct its own primary research. The organization must then choose the appropriate research approach and design the research method, whether it be a survey, focus group or interview. Only then are they ready to conduct research. Of course, after completion of the research study they must analyze and report the findings.

Research process

- What to ask: Research question.
- Whom to ask: Research subjects.
- How to ask: Research method.

Research question

The research question asks what the organization needs to know and what it currently does not know. Research questions that start with "who," "how many" or "how often" will use a quantitative descriptive research methodology such as a survey. After all there can only be a limited number of possible responses to questions about demographic characteristics, such as age, or geographic characteristics, such as home location. A research question that starts with the words "why" or "how" will usually result in a qualitative exploratory research methodology. Such questions are usually very broadly stated such as, "Why do visitors to our history reenactments not attend again?" Another exploratory research question would be, "How can we better communicate the benefits of attendance to our garden festival to younger visitors?" There could be many possible answers to these questions, which is why an exploratory technique such as focus groups or interviews will be used.

A well-written research question will be as specific as possible. It will not only provide information on what needs to be known, but will also provide information on what type of visitor will provide the information. If possible, it should also quantify any information on demographics, quantity of usage or price. For example, rather than state a research question as, "How much can prices be increased?" it should be stated as, "Will a 10 percent increase in family ticket prices negatively affect attendance?"

This very specific research question does not happen at the first attempt. Instead it will take many attempts at writing the question before it is specific enough. This process is best conducted by more than one person, so they can challenge each other over what is specifically being asked. A research question will start as broadly defining the question but successive rewrites will clarify the meaning.

Using descriptive and exploratory research

One of the questions that an organization must decide on before conducting research is which research approach will be most appropriate. The approach chosen will depend on the research question and the type of information the organization is seeking. The two general research approaches are descriptive quantitative and exploratory qualitative. The challenge is getting the right balance between the two (Asiedu 2019). It may seem that a quick and inexpensive survey is the right choice of method, but not if it doesn't provide you with the needed information.

Descriptive quantitative research

An organization will conduct descriptive research when it needs to obtain specific details on its visitors and their behavior. Descriptive research is used when statistical data are needed to answer a question. The tool used to conduct descriptive research is almost always surveys. Descriptive survey data can give answers such as "37 percent of our visitors are over the age of 55" or "28 percent of our visitors attend annually."

Descriptive quantitative research is used to find facts about potential and current visitors. It will ask questions about demographics such as age, gender, family status, income and education. Questions could also be asked about geographic location. Event preferences can be ascertained by asking visitors to choose from a list of activities or venue sites the visitors prefer. If a sufficient number of participants are involved in the study, it can even say that a fact is correct for the entire group of visitors with a high level of accuracy.

Surveys ask all research participants the same questions and to select an answer from a prepared list. The use of surveys as the only method of research is unfortunate. The type of information that surveys can provide is limited as participants are not able to answer the question with their own words. The preselected answers may not be what they would say if given the choice. Another reason for rethinking dependence on descriptive surveys is that it is increasingly difficult to find a sufficient number of people who are willing to respond. Because people are often pressed for time, and also because of privacy issues, it is difficult to motivate people to respond to a survey by email, on social media or even in person.

Because the standard research method for descriptive research is a survey, the amount of information that can be gathered is limited. For example, a survey question might ask event preference and then list four types such as food, sports, nature and music. There are two problems with getting information using a survey. First, the answers that are given as choices may not include the visitor's preferred activity, which might be history. Second, it is difficult to write survey questions that reveal why a type of activity is preferred. This is because the survey taker may not have given much thought as to why they chose to attend. Of course, the organization could give every possible answer but then the survey would be too long and not be completed.

Exploratory qualitative research

Organizations should use exploratory qualitative research when a research question requires finding information on visitor attitudes, opinions and beliefs. Exploratory research uses open-ended questions. The research methods available to conduct exploratory studies include focus groups and interviews. Exploratory research is designed to let participants provide their own answers. The research question, rather than asking for facts, focuses on the opinions and preferences of visitors. Because so many different answers will result, statistically provable answers cannot be generated, but exploratory qualitative studies, if designed with considerable thought as to what information is wanted and how it is to be obtained, can provide invaluable insights to an organization. Such a study may be large and complex or it can be conducted on a small scale. Either way, the visitor information received will provide details and insights that will help an organization adapt the event activities, price, promotion and venue to meet visitor desires.

Combining both types

While surveys are the most common form of consumer research, instead of starting with a survey, the research process should start with qualitative research methods such as focus groups and interviews to explore the issue of concern. Once this is done, a quantitative survey can be conducted to confirm the answer to the issue. Qualitative research has as its aim the discovery of the rationale for visitor behavior. For example, the research question might ask what would motivate the visitor to an event to stay in the community longer. Focus groups and interviews would be used to conduct this exploratory research. The focus group will be asked general open-ended questions so that participants can express in their own words what would motivate them. There may be many reasons why visitors might not stay longer, including cost, lack of interest or busy work schedules. If a survey is written by the organization before qualitative research is conducted, the survey might not include in their prepared answer list what is uncovered in a focus group.

If a focus group is conducted first, the insights provided by participants can be used to write the survey questions and answers. By conducting both qualitative and quantitative research, the organization can learn how to design an event to meet expectations. Both of these methods can be conducted entirely on social media or using another online method.

Research methods

- Descriptive research: Use when details on characteristics and volume are needed.
  - Example: Tourist demographics, such as age, or frequency of visits to event.
- Exploratory research: Use when seeking insights on motivation behavior.
  - Example: Motivation for travel or attitude toward the event promotion.

Finding research participants

One of the questions the tourism organization faces when deciding to conduct research is which potential or current visitors should be asked to participate. The word "population" is commonly used to define everyone of interest who could possibly be included in a research study. Researchers may define a population by geographic area and only involve participants from a specific area or within a range of the community. In addition, they may also define a population using such demographic data as age, gender, family status or ethnicity. Because the event has been designed with a specific target market based on psychographic factors, researchers may also define a population based on interests, values or lifestyles. These variables can also be used in combination. The resulting population may be very large, such as young people who attend concerts, or very small, such as people over the age of 70 who are interested at attending a dance festival. From within the population, a sample of people will be chosen to participate. If the population is too large, it will be difficult to conduct research; if it is too small, there won't be enough people to involve.

Rather than try to ask everyone within a population, most research will involve the sampling of a few people within the group. Asking everyone in the population will simply take too much time and money. Sampling of a population can be done based on probability or nonprobability.

Probability sampling

Probability sampling is used when deciding on participants for surveys. It uses techniques that result in an ability to calculate exactly the probability of a single person in a population being chosen to participate. This probability is based on the number of total people in the sample divided by the number of total people in the population. If the population is a known number, this is quite easy to calculate. A survey that includes

250 people, out of a population of 1,000, means that every individual in the population has a 25 percent probability of being included.

Of course, for most research studies the total number of people who are in a population at any given moment is unknown. For example, even at a university it is impossible to know exactly how many students are attending classes based on the last registration list. Since that list was compiled, students may have withdrawn or new students may have transferred in. There may also be students who have stopped attending classes but have not yet notified the university. Probability sampling can still be conducted with the probability calculated based on a reasonable estimate of the entire population. Most organizations will choose a random sample of a specific number of research subjects from among all the available participants.

Non-probability sampling

Qualitative research studies use nonrandom sampling methods. Nonrandom means that each potential research subject does not have the same likelihood of being chosen. However, nonrandom does not mean haphazard. Thought must be given to a process of choosing participants for any research study, even the smallest qualitative focus group or individual interviews. If fact, it could be argued that organizations conducting small qualitative studies must use extra care when choosing research subjects as so much weight will be given to the opinions of each.

The three basic methods that an organization can use when selecting participants for qualitative research studies are convenience, snowballing and purposive. A participant profile is developed that describes the characteristics of the desired research subjects. After the participant profile has been developed the organization must choose which of the three methods is most appropriate. Convenience sampling uses the participants that meet the profile and are the most convenient or easy to find. Snowballing uses recommendations after the first participant is chosen. With purposive sampling, the participants that best meet the profile are chosen.

Conducting descriptive surveys

Too often organizations will simply decide at a meeting to do a survey without adequately understanding the need to follow a process. If a survey is to effectively help answer the research question, time and thought must be put into deciding what questions will be asked. Once the questions and possible answers are decided a draft survey will then be written that will be reviewed by everyone involved. Possible issues that may arise include having too many questions so that some must be deleted. Or it may be noticed that an important topic area was not included and new questions must be added. Some questions may be found to be confusing and must be rewritten. The suggested answers may also not be the ones that may most often be chosen by the participants. In this case, the answers must be rewritten. Once the draft survey has been modified it must again be reviewed. It is not unusual for a survey to go through the writing and review process several times. Each time there should be fewer modifications. While the researchers may have felt the first draft asked exactly what was needed, they may be amazed by how much improvement will result from the review and rewrite process.

Not only do researchers need to understand the general guidelines for writing questions, they must also learn the different types of answer formats that can be used. The types are differentiated by the way that the question can be answered. Two of the most common are multiple choice and open-ended questions where the answer will be written or typed in. The advantage to open-ended questions is that the participant is allowed to answer in any way they chose. The disadvantage is that each answer will need to be read rather than a percentage being calculated. The next step is to consider the layout of the questionnaire. The design, or "look," of the survey is important as it actually affects the response rate. A poorly designed survey form can look confusing or intimidating. As a result the participant may decide not to even attempt the survey.

After the survey questions and answers have been written and approved and the layout designed, the survey is ready to be tested. The testing should be done with people who will be similar to those who will be taking the survey. For example, the form should not be tested on the organization's employees if the research participants will be of a different educational level or ethnicity. Even age can be a factor as the use of terms used by young people may be different from what is used by those from an older generation. The testing should also be conducted using the same survey method. An online survey should be tested by participants completing the form online.

Online surveys

Online survey software is available for free unless a large number of lengthy surveys need to be sent. The software programs are very intuitive and do not require extensive training. They usually provide tutorials on the use of the program. The tourism organization will still need to consider carefully the questions and answers, but writing each into the software is easy as templates are provided. Once the survey research is completed, the software will provide statistics showing the findings of all research participants, but it is still necessary for the researcher to have a basic understanding of what the statistics mean.

Social media and texting surveys

Surveys can be distributed to research subjects using email, which allows the researcher to individually choose each potential participant. The body of the email is used to explain the reason for the survey and contains a link to the survey site. To motivate participation a well-written email should explain that the results of the survey will assist in producing a better event experience for future visitors. The problem with this method of distribution is that it is limited to people for which the organization has an email address. These are most likely people who have already visited or at least have requested information on the destination.

Another means of obtaining research participants is to send out text messages to the research sample with a link to the survey. Surveys that are texted now receive a higher response rate than emailed surveys (Kassabov 2019). This method works well with participants who already have a close relationship with the organization. The text message does not allow the researcher to communicate any lengthy information that would motivate participation. Response to the survey request can be increased by including a message that the first 100 people who respond and complete the survey will receive an entrance ticket discount or other small incentive.

Social media is a third technology that can be used as a means to distribute the survey to a wider range of research participants. The organization should only post on social media sites on which it is already active and has a following. These followers have demonstrated that they are interested in what the destination has to offer. If the survey is going to posted or tweeted it should be short. Even if the link brings the research participant to the survey software, people on social media are rarely interested in spending time answering questions. It may be necessary to offer an incentive for completing the survey form. As the people who are on the organization's social media sites are interested in the destination, providing a discount should motivate completion. Another idea is to enter all those who complete the survey into a contest where the prize is a free trip to the event. This method has the advantage is reaching a wide variety of respondents, particularly if participants are asked to share the link with friends.

Conducting exploratory focus groups and interviews

The organization should conduct exploratory research studies when they need information on visitors' feelings, values and attitudes. While descriptive studies will provide facts about visitors, only exploratory studies can answer the question of why visitors choose to attend an event. Exploratory studies, which include focus groups and interviews, are also useful in uncovering social changes in visitor motivation and their attitudes toward events. Because the visitors themselves may be largely unaware of their motivation, a simple survey question is unable to determine this information.

Because visitor motivation varies, many different answers will be obtained for each question posed during a survey or interview. For this reason, qualitative exploratory research does not provide statistical facts. The answers obtained will be much more detailed and informative than the data that is obtained from a survey. When analyzing qualitative data, instead of being just counted, responses are grouped by theme or frequency. For example the study may find that a desire for family activities or live music was a theme that was often mentioned by participants in focus groups. It is these themes rather than each individual response that will be included in the research report.

Exploratory research is qualitative rather than quantitative, which means the quality of the answers is more important than how many participants respond to the question. Using a qualitative approach means that fewer participants will be involved in the research. However more time will be needed to conduct the research because more time is spent with each participant. The questions will take more time because they will ask the participants questions on their motivation that cannot be quickly or easily answered.

Focus groups

Focus groups are a qualitative research technique that uses participant interaction to uncover attitudes, opinions and values. Focus groups are considered exploratory research because an issue or problem is being explored. For this reason focus groups are often one of the first choices when little is known about the cause of a problem such as a decrease in attendance. Once focus groups have been used as a first step in exploring an issue, the findings can be confirmed using a quantitative research technique such as a survey.

Focus groups are sometimes misunderstood as mere discussions where people just talk while a moderator listens. However, a well-designed focus group conducted by a skilled moderator is much more than that. The purpose of a focus group is to encourage participants to go beyond their first response to the issue being discussed. Interaction with the moderator and also between the group members is designed to uncover deeper insights which can be used to develop new and creative ideas for solutions to problems. Focus groups do not start with an assumption about the cause of a problem. Instead, they are used to generate new ideas for the organization. A focus group can generate ideas for new event activities, a different type of venue and more effective promotional message. In addition, they can be used to explore reasons for an event's problems or failures.

The process of planning a focus group starts by deciding what issues should be covered during the group and then writing focus group questions. During the focus group session the questions should start with the easiest and then progress to the more difficult. It is important that the questions stay focused. An hour-long focus group session with eight participants does not result in eight hours of discussion, but only one. In addition, the focus group topics must be related. If a focus group is to be successful, it cannot jump from one topic to another. It takes time to develop the rapport that makes the participants willing to discuss challenging issues.

After the focus group discussion topics have been chosen, the next step in the process is to decide who will be involved in the focus group. Because many fewer participants will be involved than in a survey, it is especially important that the correct participants be chosen. Choosing an appropriate moderator is also important. A larger organization may have someone on staff that can perform this function. However, it may be necessary to recruit someone from outside the organization to perform this task.

The first part of the focus group is used to build rapport between the moderator and the participants. The first questions asked should be easy ones that pertain to experiences or knowledge all of the participants share. Starting the focus group with challenging questions may intimidate the participants and result in less interaction throughout the remainder of the group session. It is the moderator's responsibility to encourage active participation while at the same time not making any of the participants feel pressured to speak. This is the "art" that the moderator performs that may not be understood by others. The moderator must watch and assess the facial expressions of any quiet group members to gauge when will be the right time to encourage them to speak. By keeping the early questions easy to answer and non-threatening and encouraging everyone to speak, the moderator prepares the participants for more challenging questions later in the focus group.

Either the session will be recorded of someone will be assigned to take careful notes. The analysis stage of the focus group methodology involves transcribing the tapes and organizing the notes. Once this has been completed, the moderator will analyze the information for themes. After the themes have been analyzed, the moderator will write the report and make a presentation.

Interviews

Tourism, hospitality and event organizations will certainly know that much can be learned about the needs of their visitors by informally asking about their experiences. However, most tourism organizations have not considered using interviews in a more formal way for visitor research. They should reconsider this attitude as interviews can be very useful and worth the investment in time, effort and money when the organization is faced with a serious problem, such as a lack of visitors or a recent uptick in online bad reviews for which they do not know the cause.

Interview research consists of the researcher asking questions of a single participant. Some of the questions will be predetermined while follow-up questions will be added when needed during the process. In-depth interviews conducted with visitors are often used to uncover the source of a problem. To do so the interviewer should encourage storytelling from personal experience rather than just the statement of facts (McNiff 2017). The longer time spent with the subject will allow the researcher time to gain insights that having only a short conversation would not be able to produce. The insights from interviews can be used to better understand a current problem that is confronting the organization. For example, an event that is seeing a decline in visitors may use interviews to get a deeper understanding of the reason for this decline than can be obtained from survey responses. If the numerous survey responses mention a lack of interesting activities, interviews can be used to determine how the activities could be changed to be considered fun. Surveys are not always reliable as participants may not take time to consider their responses (Kenny 2019). A skilled interview will probe beyond this first response.

While in-depth interviews can be used to gain insights from visitors into the cause of a problem, intercept interviews allow the researcher to quickly gather opinions from many visitors of their impression of a tourism product or service. For example, a tourism organization may conduct intercept interviews as visitors are leaving an event. The visitors may be asked why they visited and if they plan to return. Many may state that the cost of tickets is too expensive for a return visit, while others may state that there is little to do at the site. These reasons could then be further explored using survey research.

Expert interviews are held with subjects other than visitors. Instead expert interviews are usually conducted with competitors and provide a means of gathering factual information. This includes information from other organizations that have faced a similar difficulty. For example, if organizers of a music festival know that there is higher attendance at other festivals, they may want to interview managers at the competing event to determine how they attract visitors.

It is true that an in-depth interview takes a skilled interviewer and, therefore, might not be a methodology that is available to small organizations. However, all organizations can have their own personnel conduct expert interviews to learn more about their competition and then adjust their marketing mix accordingly. In addition, intercept interviews can be conducted by anyone with an outgoing personality and these will provide the organization with insights that can be confirmed with other research techniques.

Discussion questions

1. How can we learn what benefits visitors want from attending an event?
2. Why should a process be followed when conducting research?
3. What is the difference between quantitative descriptive research and qualitative exploratory research?
4. How can two types of research be combined?
5. How are participants for research selected?
6. What are the advantages of using surveys?
7. Why should the organization write their own survey questions?
8. How can surveys be linked to social media?
9. Why should focus groups and interviews be conducted to understand the emotional motivation for attendance?
10. What is the reason for holding in-depth interviews?

Case

Online focus groups need a bit of adjustment

Online focus groups, once a rarity, are growing in popularity. Potential research subjects are less willing to come to a central location to participate due to time constraints. They may also be unable to travel because of health or disability limitations. Having online focus groups is more convenient and participants can be from a wider geographic area. However an online focus group does require some adjustment from the traditional methodology.

- Smaller: Because it can be harder for people to stay engaged online, only four to five people should be involved rather than the traditional seven to nine. This will also allow everyone's face to be shown on screen.
- Shorter: The time for the group should be limited to no more than 90 minutes with a limit of three topics to be covered. Because it is easy for participants to be distracted, the moderator must ensure that everyone participates.
- Tech: Participants should be sent an email with a link to the software that will be used so they can gain familiarity. This can even involve a test session at the time of the participant choosing so that the software can be tried live.
- Contact: Participants should be given the phone number of a tech contact in case they have difficulties in getting or staying connected. This should not be the moderator but someone skilled in teaching people how to use technology.
- Engagement: Use a software platform that allows posting and sharing of information that arises during brainstorming. Short questions can be posted that everyone answers can also increase participation (UXalliance 2020).

Task: What would be the advantage to my event to conduct an online focus group?

Case

Survey results should lead to actions

There are numerous sources of information on how to write survey questions. In fact many programs for developing online surveys will include tutorials on the subject. However there is less information on how to use the answers once the survey is completed. Here is a process for turning survey results into useable ideas.

- Really look: Don't think you already know the answers. It is very tempting to look for the answers you want, and by doing so, miss important facts.
- Review all the results: Instead of only looking at overall total responses to questions, scroll through all the responses. This will give you a broader view of the range of results.

- Look for unusual responses: After the overview, it is time to look at the percentage of different responses to each question. It is natural to look at the responses that ranked high, but keep an open mind, and eye, for the outlying responses. They can inform you of issues that could become more critical in the future.
- Use statistical analysis: Your survey program can generate much more than just total number of responses and percentages. Learn how to use and understand cross tabulations as they can show relationships between answers.
- Create visuals: Many people find it easier to understand numbers when they are in charts or graphs. They also provide a more dramatic effect if data is widely skewed in one direction.
- Determine action: If all that is done with survey results is to analyze and report the findings, the survey has been a waste of time and money. Instead, action based on the findings should be recommended (Stillwagon 2017).

Task: Look at at least two online survey creation platforms to see what type of data analysis they can produce for your event.

Event plan: Use the information from this chapter to complete the first section of the event plan outline at the end of the book.

References

Asiedu, Felicia. 2019. "Qualitative vs. Quantitative Research Methods for Your Event." *Cvent*. May 30, 2019. https://www.cvent.com/uk/blog/hospitality/qualitative-vs-quantitative-research-methods-event. November 5, 2020.

Beaulac, Hugh. 2019. "How to Use Social Media for Market Research." *CXL Institute*. February 18, 2019. https://cxl.com/blog/social-media-market-research/. Accessed September 2, 2020.

Kaemingk, Diana. 2018. "6 Ways Disney World Delivers Top Customer Experiences." *Qualtrics XM*. October 2, 2018. https://www.qualtrics.com/blog/6-ways-disney-world-delivers-top-customer-experiences/. Accessed December 6, 2020.

Kassabov, Kalin. 2019. "How to Get the Most Out of Customer Polls and Surveys." *Forbes*. December 19, 2019. https://www.forbes.com/sites/theyec/2019/12/09/how-to-get-the-most-out-of-customer-polls-and-surveys/#4d2948e46f92. Accessed September 30, 2020.

Kenny, Graham. 2019. "Customer Surveys Are No Substitute for Actually Talking to Customers." *Harvard Business Review*. January 17, 2019. https://hbr.org/2019/01/customers-surveys-are-no-substitute-for-actually-talking-to-customers. Accessed October 2, 2020.

McNiff, Kath. 2017. "Are You Really Listening? Tips for Conducting Qualitative Interviews." *NVIVO*. April 25, 2017. https://www.qsrinternational.com/nvivo-qualitative-data-analysis-software/resources/blog/tips-for-conducting-qualitative-interviews. Accessed November 7, 2020.

Stillwagon, Amanda. 2017. "How to Analyze and Interpret Survey Results." *Small Business Trends*. December 16, 2017. https://smallbiztrends.com/2014/11/how-to-interpret-survey-results.html Accessed November 7, 2020.

UXalliance. 2020. "Conducting Remote Online Focus Groups in Times of Covid-19." *UXalliance*. April 4, 2020. https://uxalliance.medium.com/conducting-remote-online-focus-groups-in-times-of-covid-19-ee1c66644fdb. Accessed October 21, 2020.

Chapter 6

Developing the budget and setting the price

Abstract

The organization must decide the financial objective of the event, which might be to break even or make a profit. The event may need to be subsidized by other revenue sources in order to break even. If the event is expected to make a profit, revenue must be greater than expenses. Sponsorships may be needed if revenue is insufficient. Before a price can be set, fixed and variable costs should be determined. The price to attend should be set to cover both. It could also be set by matching a competitor's price. Prestige pricing is used for exclusive events. Budgets must be used to control expenses which should be listed separately by type. Revenue should also be tracked by source including tickets, product sales and sponsorships. The budget should be continually referenced throughout the planning process. To cover expenses, additional sources of revenue besides tickets sales should be explored. Vendors might be allowed to sell products to visitors. Methods of payments need to be explored and a point-of-sale method set up. After the event, the variance between projected expenses and revenue are compared with what was actually spent and received.

Expenses and revenue

When an event is in the early stages of development, the discussion will focus on how to attract visitors. There will be discussions about the event objectives such as enhancing the reputation of the community and generating goodwill among residents. Simply stating that gaining awareness of the goodwill of the community is not sufficient as a goal (Modern Tribe 2019). This is because there is no way to measure and quantify if success has been achieved.

Financial goals

The planning process needs to include financial goals that can be measured and quantified. A tourism event may be designed to bring in sufficient revenue to make a profit, even if the organization sponsoring the event is a nonprofit. The surplus funds generated by the event may be needed to fund other expenses such as the development of a tourism website or funding of the visitor center. A different objective would be to just make enough money to cover costs so that no additional funds are needed. Lastly it might be anticipated that there will not be enough revenue to even cover costs. The event may still be held with the belief that more visitors will be attracted in the future. The tourism organization might use existing funds in their budget to cover the costs not covered by event revenue. If they do not have the funds, the organization would need to look for funding from other sources such as sponsorships.

A lodging company may decide to hold an event on their own. As a profit-making business they will state that their goal is to sell a certain number of rooms. They may decide to price the room nights low just to cover costs if the event is held at a time in the year when bookings are low. They would do so in the hope that attendees would return at another time of the year and pay more for a room. If the event is very popular, room nights will be booked at a higher rate.

Whether the objective is to generate a profit, simply cover costs, or find additional funding, the numbers for revenue and expenses must be projected early during the planning stages. Even if some of the event components do not cost the organization anything, such as volunteer staff, it needs to be known if there are funds to cover other expected expenses. There is no point in planning for a prestige venue with gourmet catering if there will be no money to pay the costs.

Financial objectives for events

- Profit: Surplus funds reinvested in organization.
- Cover costs: Make enough revenue to cover expenses, so no loss.
- External support: Use funds from other sources to cover expenses.

Relationship between price, revenue and profit

Except for those working in finance, most people working in tourism and hospitality do not often consider the relationship between price, revenue, expenses and profit. Everyone knows that price is what is charged for the product. It is an exchange of value where the consumer is willing to give up some of their wealth in payment for a product that will solve a problem or meet a need. If price is multiplied by the number of items sold, revenue is calculated. Often revenue figures are what are discussed by organizations. Revenue for hotels and other tourism companies are often quoted in the business news. Event managers may brag about the revenue generated by an event. A high revenue figure is often used positively to show the success of a company or event. The belief is that if a business has a high level of revenue, then it must be doing well. In fact, the revenue figure is only evidence that the product is being sold; it is not evidence of the financial success of the event. Rather than revenue, it is the level of profit, revenue minus expenses, that demonstrates if the event has been successful. Even if the financial objective is simply to break even by covering costs, projecting and tracking revenue and expenses is critical.

Total revenue is calculated by first adding together the money received from ticket sales with other sources such as sales of souvenirs and refreshments. Revenue may have also been received from sponsorships or grants. Total expenses would include not just expenses that relate directly to the event, such as venue rental and food costs, but would also include staffing and marketing. Total expenses are then subtracted from total revenue. If the final number is zero, the event has broken even, meaning no money was made but also none was lost. If the number is positive, the event has made a profit, while if the number is negative, there has been a financial loss. It is possible to have a loss even when the event was well attended and many other products were sold. If the costs are too high, a loss will still result. Everyone probably knows someone who makes a good income but is still broke at the end of the month because he or she has spent too much money; the same is true of any business. It is only the money that is left after paying the expenses that is a profit.

When an event that is supposed to make a profit is projected not to do so, the solution may seem simple. After all, if prices are raised, total revenue will be increased. Unfortunately, this simple solution is not necessarily effective; the rise in price may be offset by fewer people attending the event as some people refuse to purchase at the higher price. It may then seem that a reduction in price is the best way to increase profit as it would raise revenue because more people would attend. However, the organization needs to be careful using this strategy because while more products may be sold, any increase in product sold will be offset by less revenue being received as all the tickets are now being sold at the lower price.

If prices cannot be raised and should not be lowered, then the other solution to increase profit is to cut expenses. This strategy is certainly something that must be considered. However, cutting expenses may also adversely affect the attendance at the event. For example, if the decision is made to move the event to a less expensive venue to cut expenses, fewer people may be interested in attending. If less expensive entertainment is hired, it might result in changing the image of the event and visitors not being willing to pay the same price. Pricing to generate the maximum revenue, while keeping expenses to a minimum so as generate a profit, is more difficult than it might first appear.

Setting the price

The organization might be tempted to charge a low price for the event so as to attract attendance. The problem is that once a price for a product is established, it is difficult to change as consumers will be unhappy with price increases. Therefore, getting the price correct when it is first introduced is critical. Only after the difference between fixed and variable costs are understood can the product be correctly priced.

Fixed and variable costs

Fixed costs are those that would need to be paid whether or not any tickets are sold or visitors attend. Common terms for such costs are overhead or operating expenses. Keeping fixed costs low is critical for two reasons. First, fixed costs must be paid in full whether the event is well or poorly attended, which makes an event with high fixed costs vulnerable to failure. Many events may not attract a large audience the first time they are held. It may take time before the event gains a positive reputation and the visitor numbers increase substantially. The risk is that if the event loses money the first year, it may never be held again. The second reason for keeping fixed costs low is that they affect the ticket price. The lower the fixed costs, the lower the tickets can be priced.

Fixed costs would include any bill that must be paid even if no one attends. If a venue is leased for the event, the contract will state that the bill must be paid in full no matter what amount of revenue is received. In addition, paying for utility costs, permit fees and equipment rental are inescapable. The companies that provide these services have committed time and resources and must pay for their own costs. For large events, if the services cannot be done by existing staff, contracts for security and janitorial services will have been signed. Again, the contracts will require payment even if the services have been used by only a few visitors. Vehicles and equipment used in production of the event would also be fixed costs. Because fixed costs must be paid even if few people attend it is critical for the events success that these costs are kept as low as possible.

Variable costs are ones that increase with each attendee. They are called variable because the total amount of costs will vary depending on how many people attend. If food and beverage are provided, the cost will increase based on the number of attendees that need to be fed. If gift bags or souvenirs are provided for each attendee this would be another variable cost. Most of the costs involved with events are fixed which makes keeping them under control critical.

Breakeven analysis

Keeping track of expenses might seem less exciting then planning the event. However, doing so will help the organization meet its financial goal. All bills must be paid, if not directly from visitor revenue, then from another source. One way to think about the relationship between expenses and ticket price is breakeven analysis. To calculate the breakeven point all fixed expenses, whether paid before the event or after its conclusion, are added together. The second step is to calculate the total variable expenses that must be paid per visitor. For example, the total fixed expenses for the event might be €10,000 or any other currency. The variable expenses might be €10 per person. The organization might decide on a ticket price of €30. For each €30 ticket sold, the organization only makes €20 after subtracting the variable expenses. For the first tickets sold, the €20 must be applied to cover the fixed costs. It will take 500 people attending the event paying €30, only €20 of which can be applied to cover the fixed costs. The organization receives no money as profit until the person 501 buys a ticket. Even then, the organization only makes €20 profit from each additional ticket as €10 from each ticket must be used to cover variable expenses. This calculation tells us that if the goal is just to break even, 500 tickets must be sold. If the goal is to make €20,000, 1,500 tickets must be sold.

Breakeven analysis

- Fixed costs: Must be paid even if no tickets are sold.
- Variable costs: Costs incurred for each person attending.
- Breakeven: Number of tickets that must be sold before fixed costs are covered.

Cost pricing

When deciding on the price of a product, one of the first issues that must be considered is the actual cost of producing the product. To be profitable, the price charged must at least cover both the fixed costs of the event and the variable costs that result from each attendee. There is no difference in pricing a for-profit and nonprofit event. In both cases the costs must be paid for. The difference is how any profit after costs are covered is handled. For a for-profit business event, the profit can be used in any way, including the personal expenses of the business owners. If the organization hosting the event is a non-profit, the profit must be used to further the mission of the organization or be set aside to cover any future losses. After determining the fixed and variable costs of producing the product, the organization can start with the number of people expected to attend and then charge a price that will cover both types of costs. Any additional amount from attendees then generates a surplus of revenue or profit.

Competitive pricing

Because of the difficulty in calculating the actual costs of producing a service product, such as an event, there are other pricing methods that can be used. One of the simplest is to use similar competing events as a guide. Potential visitors will expect the ticket price to be comparable with similar events that are held. If the price for other events is higher, then even a slightly lower price will be perceived as good value by the potential visitor (Sandeep, Mewborn and Caine 2017). However it is not always easy to find the appropriate event for comparison. This is particularly true in the case of a small community-based event. In this case, the competition may not be other events but how a potential visitor might otherwise spend their money that day, such as taking the family to an amusement park.

If the organizers are using competition pricing, they must still also consider the event costs. The further the price it charges is from the price that would allow the organization to cover all costs, that is, the breakeven point, the more reliant the organizer must be on having other sources of income.

Prestige pricing

If the event organizer cannot price directly on cost, or price their tickets the same as competitors, there is another method of pricing. For some specialty events, for which there is no easily obtained substitute, the event can price high and still attract attendees. The organization can price the ticket higher by promoting the prestige value of the event (Smith 2019). This is the value that the potential visitor believes they will receive from attendance.

Visitors are willing to pay high prices for prestige value because they know that they will be given the opportunity to experience an event that is rarely available. Besides being able to attend the event, they are also purchasing the ability to enhance their status by posting online photos and using other social media sites to boast of their experience.

Varying pricing by visitor segment

At first it might not seem fair, but there are good reasons why everyone should not be charged the same price. Pricing may be discounted for groups, families or targeted individuals, or varied based on time of day or date of attendance. When people are bringing a group to an event, they may very well expect a discount. It takes marketing expense to attract visitors. It costs less for the organization to sell ten tickets at once than attract ten different visitors buying one ticket each. For this reason, tickets may be discounted for group sales. If the event wishes to attract families, the larger the family, the higher the total price for attendance, which could keep some families from attending. Charging a family price will not only allow more families to attend but will generate good will. Good will can also be the result of discounts for military veterans, the elderly or people on benefits. It may not guarantee additional attendance but will be viewed favorably by the public.

Another differential pricing idea is to charge less for tickets that are purchased early. This can bring in early revenue that can be used to pay bills. If the event is held for more than a day, a discounted ticket might be offered to multi-day visitors. The longer visitors are at the event the more additional money they will spend on products such as souvenirs and food. To increase support for the event from the community, another idea is to sell discounted tickets to local residents. If tickets are sold on site, they can be asked for identification that shows they live in the community. A variation of differential pricing is a "pay what you can" day at the event. This might be the last day of a multi-day event when attendance slows. Or, it could be late in the day at the end of the event. Even if the visitor decides to not pay anything, they may still spend money on food or products.

Differential pricing can also be used to encourage ticket sales during slow attendance periods. If early mornings or late evenings have fewer visitors, ticket prices can be lowered when used during these time periods. While doing so will generate less revenue, since attendance was low anyway, any additional revenue will be welcomed. The same strategy can be used for days of the week when attendance is lower. When using differential pricing, the word "discount" should not be used as it has a negative connotation and suggests a lowering of quality. Instead, the price differential should be expressed as an extra savings for family or a recognition of service, such as for the military.

Pricing strategies

- Cost: Setting price to cover fixed and variable costs.
- Competitive: Price is comparable to similar events.
- Prestige: Price is high because of status and exclusivity.
- Special: Pricing varies based on type of buyer.

Price elasticity and pricing

An economic term, price elasticity, call help event organizers think through pricing issues. This term refers to how sensitive the consumer is to a change in prices. Inelastic products are ones where the demand does not change even if the price is increased by a large amount. These are usually products that are needed immediately or in an emergency. Elastic-priced products are ones where a small change in price results in a large change in demand. These are products where lower-priced competing products can be easily be purchased. Most products are in-between these two extremes.

What is important for event organizers to remember is that an increase or decrease in ticket price will affect attendance. The organization may believe that a 10 percent rise in ticket price will increase revenue by 10 percent, but this is not true. The revenue from the higher ticket price may be more than offset by a decrease in the number of tickets sold. A higher ticket price may result in a financial loss rather than gain. Likewise, a decrease in ticket price means that more attendance will be needed to make up for lost revenue. While it may be impossible to know exactly how a change in price will affect demand, it is critical to remember that a change in price is not a quick fix for increasing revenue or attendance.

Creating the budget

Preparing and then following a budget are essential steps in ensuring a successful event. Budgets are first used to project future expenses so that they can be matched against projected future revenue. Using a budget is not an optional activity but rather the only means of ensuring that the bills can be paid. No matter what the attendance figure, if the event loses money and the bills aren't paid, it can't be considered a success.

All types of organizations and businesses are often surprised by the amount of expenses that occur even before the date of the event. Rent for a venue is often due up front along with a deposit to secure the contracts of entertainers and caters. Even if the full amount is not due, deposits must be paid. The organization must either limit the amount that must be paid out before the event or have a means of ensuring that funds are available during event planning. If tickets are sold before the event occurs this can help with meeting expenses. Likewise, if sponsorship money can also be paid before the event, this can help. If not, the organization will need internal funds available to be cover upfront expenses.

Revenue accounts

There are a number of revenue sources that should be explored by the organizations involved in planning the event. Of course, ticket sales could be an important source. However, not all events are designed as ticketed events. There are still sources of revenue that could offset expenses including product sales, charging for additional activities, and food and beverage sales. There should be separate tracking in the budget for every type of revenue that is received so that the total available amount is known.

One of the most difficult tasks when planning a new event is projecting future revenue. Most organizations will start with an estimate of how many people they believe will attend. They will then estimate how much each visitor will spend. They will multiply these two numbers to get an estimate on revenue. Another approach is to first start with a goal of how much money should be made. This profit goal would be enough to cover both the fixed and the variable costs of the event and ensure any required profit. The next step would then be to determine how many visitors need to attend to reach this revenue goal.

Most events will have more than one means of obtaining revenue. To both project future and track actual revenue, each of these should have a separate budget line that includes both the number of products or tickets sold and the resulting revenue. For example, there might be budget lines for ticket revenue, souvenir sales, food, tours and sponsorships.

After the completion of the event, actual revenue from the event will be tracked and then compared with what was budgeted. Some event planners might think there is no purpose to this exercise as there are so many unknowns. However, much can be learned from comparing budgeted and actual revenue. There might be categories where there is more revenue than expected and others where there is less. For example, if it is found that activities for which additional tickets were required, such as late evening events or walking tours, generated significant revenue, the organization will then know these should again be offered at the next event and might even be expanded. If activities such as dance lessons generated only a small amount of revenue, they will not be offered at the next event.

Revenue from unbundling prices

In an effort to keep ticket prices low, event organizers may wish to consider pricing some event activities separately. "Unbundling" is the idea of keeping base ticket prices low but then charging for other costs. Additional revenue could come from charging for parking or souvenir programs. Admission to VIP areas where visitors receive special attention or are closer to the entertainment are another separate pricing opportunity. Adding on a premium drinks or food package to the ticket price would also increase revenue.

More creative ways of receiving addition revenue could be holding a raffle with items donated by local businesses. They would receive publicity while the organizers would receive revenue without costs. For larger events, tickets to corporate hospitality areas could be sold. Photo booths with costumes can be a fun activity for which a small amount can be charged. Old-fashioned carnival-type games or petting zoos for which additional tickets can be sold might be considered for family events.

Revenue from vendors

Having appropriate vendors can not only bring in additional revenue, it can also enhance the visitor experience. The vendor might provide refreshments, products or experiences. Everyone will expect some type of food and beverage at an event. While the organization could provide this service themselves or hire a catering service, there are other alternatives that bring in revenue. Food vendors or food trucks can be part of the ambience of the event. Other vendors could sell products that are related to the event. For example, a gardening event could attract vendors selling plants, while a family friendly event might attract a vendor that makes handcrafted toys.

There are three types of vendors. The first are large companies that sell services, such as home renovation or insurance. They have marketing budgets that include booth rental at events. They are interested in interacting with people in their targeted customer segment. The second type of vendor are those whose main source of revenue is selling their product at events. Because this is their only source of revenue they are only interested in events with enough potential sells to make it worth their while. The third type of businesses are hobbyists. They make items such as jewelry, pottery or flower arrangements. They need to make fewer sales because they have other sources of revenue. They are interested in attending smaller event because not only will they sell products, but it is a way for them to find new customers for future sales.

Vendors are charged a fee for the opportunity to be at the event. If the event is new, an additional low-cost incentive to attract vendors is to provide a specific number of free tickets to the event for them to share with others. A contract with the vendor should be prepared with payment to be received before completion of the event.

Expense accounts

Of course, revenue is not the same as profit, as expenses will first need to be paid. For budgeting purposes, expenses also need to be divided into categories that are tracked separately. If expenses are too high, it is not enough just to say less money must be spent.

There needs to be tracking of where the money was spent so that an expense critical for the running of the event is not cut. How to categorize expenses will be unique to each type of event. However, there will probably need to be a separate account for each type of expense, such as venue rental, entertainment, security and promotion. Marketing expenses can be tracked as a single expense. If marketing expenses are large they should be divided into separate expense lines such as print advertising, posters and social media costs.

Only by using this type of budgeting will the organization know what event generates the most profit, not just revenue. For example if entertainers are hired to perform at the event, the expenses would include the fee and any other expenses such as paying for transportation and lodging. After a comparison of income to expenses it may be decided that the performances are actually losing the event money. In this situation, either the expenses incurred must be lowered or the prices raised, or, if neither of these is possible, the performances should no longer be given.

There are also expenses that it is necessary to pay that are not directly related to production of the product. These are called general and administrative expenses and they include staffing, any lease payment for office space and any vehicle maintenance expenses. Other issues not directly related to the event that should be tracked would be insurance costs, tax payments, licensing and legal expenses.

Analyzing variances

It is not enough just to create and keep a budget. After the event is over and all the bills are paid, the actual revenue, expense and profit amounts will be compared to what was budgeted. A negative variance in expenses between the budgeted amount and actual can result from higher than anticipated fixed costs, such as venue rental, or higher variable costs, such as additional money spent on free food for each attendee. These changes from the budgeted amount will either lower or raise profit. On the revenue side, a common cause of a negative variance is attendance that is lower than expected. A positive variance in revenue results when attendance goals are exceeded. Any negative variance is a warning sign that should not be ignored (Woodruff 2019). Corrective action needs to be taken the next time the event is held by lowering costs or increasing attendance.

Additional financial issues

There are two ways that expenses and revenue can be tracked. While the services of an accountant may be needed for a large event, the organization staff can perform all the bookkeeping tasks needed for a small event. There are many software packages that can help with tracking the numbers, but how and when the amounts are recorded is an issue that must be thought through.

Some costs must be paid for immediately. This could be for supplies or deposits for entertainment. Other costs will not be due until immediately during the event or even after the event has been completed. It is easy for the event organizers to forget about the bills that will need to be paid later. Likewise, some revenue, such as advance ticket sales, will be received before the event. Other revenue, such as product sales, will be received at the event while vendors may pay a percentage of sales after the event has been completed.

A system of cash accounting only records expenses and revenue when it is received. While this system is easy to maintain, it can result in overspending because not enough attention is given to what expenses are incurred but not yet paid. Accrual accounting takes into consideration what needs to be paid in the future. It records the amount that is committed even if not yet paid. While it sounds complicated, it can be as easy as simply keeping a spreadsheet with a column entitled bills to be paid. The same system can also record revenue that has been promised, but it is the bills that must be paid in the future that can result in overspending.

Finding sponsorships

In addition to the revenue sources from ticket, product and food sales, another idea is to get funding from sponsorships. They have become increasingly important as a revenue source for all types of for-profit and nonprofit events. Businesses are interested in sponsoring events as they have difficulty in getting their marketing message heard using traditional media communication methods. Sponsorship can provide the company with access to visitors who are currently unaware of the product that they offer. When visitors see that the event they enjoyed was sponsored by a company, it extends the marketing reach of the sponsor. The company may also be interested in sponsorship because they are trying to appeal to the specific target market that is attending the event.

Organizations are interested in finding sponsors because, as potential visitors have many events from which to choose, it is difficult to charge a high ticket price. The high cost of entertainment or venue may be necessary to attract attendees, but they are not willing to pay a higher ticket price to do so. Getting sponsors to provide funding for an event may be necessary when ticket and product sales do not cover expenses. Sponsorship with the right company can also enhance the image of the event.

Sponsorship is not charity. Sponsors expect a return on their investment. This might be an enhancement of their image, a chance to sell product at the event or the opportunity to market directly to event visitors. If personnel from the sponsoring company are at the event, it has been traditional to simply put them in a booth or behind a table in the hopes that visitors would walk over and engage in conversation. This rarely happens, resulting in frustrated sponsors who won't be willing to sponsor in the future. One way to solve this problem is to eliminate the booth and table (Stecker 2018). Instead, sponsors can be provided access to mix and mingle with visitors. For example, at a cooking festival, restaurant owners, cookware providers and cooking lesson schools would be able to mix with the visitors and natural conversations about the product the company provides would occur. If the visitor wanted more information, it would then be provided

Choosing the correct sponsor will depend on the mission and values of the organization holding the event and also the values of the potential visitors. Not all products may fit with the event image. Issues to consider include the political stance of the company. Companies with a clear political agenda not held by everyone may limit attendance. Other issues would be the type of product the company produces as sponsors of a controversial product targeted at adults might not be appropriate for a family-oriented event.

Payment methods

Another financial issue is to decide what payment methods will be accepted at the event. Less physical currency is being used for payments as electronic methods have become more popular. This has been a trend for a number of years but has been accelerating. Some businesses are not taking cash at all. There are two advantages for not handling cash. One is that having cash raises a security issue as it can be lost or stolen. While systems can be designed to keep cash safe from theft by a visitor, it is often the case that cash is stolen by staff members. It is quite easy for a staff member to take cash from a visitor, not ring up the sale and then keep the money. A second reason for not using cash is health concerns as the handling of currency can spread illnesses. There is concern that not accepting cash will negatively affect people without bank accounts (Quell 2020). Some countries and regions are passing legislation that mandates that cash be accepted.

Electronic methods of payment include credit cards. While there will be a fee that must be paid by the organization, most people expect to pay by card. Even easier for visitors is to use their phones to pay. The event organizers should research what type of payment method is most likely to be used by visitors as the electronic options change as technology develops. There are many point-of-sale software systems that can be used for the purchase of tickets and merchandise. All that is needed is to download software onto a tablet or even just a phone. A small device is added to each to allow for swiping the credit card. Before the event, the point-of-sale software will be set up with different revenue sources. There might be one account for single ticket sales while another account records group sales. Product sales might also be added to the account. All that is needed is to click on the correct online button and the sale will be recorded to the correct budget line. After the event, these revenue accounts will be able to be recorded into the bookkeeping system or even downloaded automatically.

Discussion questions

1. Why should the financial objective of an event be determined?
2. Why is it critical to understand that revenue is different from profit?
3. What can be done if ticket sales do not cover expenses?
4. Why would an organization be willing to pay to be a sponsor of an event?
5. What is the difference between fixed costs and variable costs?
6. When should cost, competition or prestige pricing be used?
7. Why is budgeting critical for the success of an event?
8. How are variances analyzed after an event?
9. What additional revenue sources might be obtained at the event?
10. Why does the event need a point-of-sale system?

Case

What to include in a budget

It can be overwhelming when you start to build a budget. There are so many different expenses that will need to be included. If they are not, when the bills come due, the expected profit while not happen. One way to start to build your expenses for the budget is to first think in categories that will then be broken down into specific lines. How much should you spend? One way to think about the issue is to prioritize the categories listed and assign a percentage of budget to each. Remember to leave 5–10 percent in the contingency category as there will always be cost over-runs of surprise expenses. Some ideas for categories are the following.

- Experience: This category will vary based on the type of experience that needs to be provided but will include fees, housing and transportation costs of speakers, entertainers, activities and music groups.
- Technology: This would include the rental or purchase of sound and lighting equipment, ticketing software, app development, and livestreaming.
- Venue: This category covers more than just the venue rental price as it also needs to cover tables and seating, dance flooring, décor, linens, decoration and security costs.
- Promotion: This category needs to be higher for a new event as it must build awareness and would include advertisement placement, sales incentives, social media sites and printed material.
- Contingency fund: Have at least 5 percent, and even better, 10 percent, in your budget to cover the unexpected (Sawyer 2019).

Task: List your budget categories by importance and give a percentage of spending to each.

Case

Get creative with pricing

Everyone worries about setting prices: too high and people won't attend; too low and you can't cover costs. But pricing isn't about setting a single price. It is easier to think of a base price and then get creative. Here are some ways that pricing can be manipulated to increase sales.

- Introductory pricing: If the event is new, start with a low introductory price. But make sure you promote that this is only for a short time period.
- Create tired pricing: Just as airlines do, have various prices for the same core product but then include add-ons for higher prices. Suddenly your lowest price seemed even lower by comparison.
- Psychological pricing: A ticket price of 49 is only slightly cheaper than 50. But it then can be promoted that tickets are less than 50!
- Additional tickets: If tickets sales are low, go back to people who have purchased and offer them discounted tickets for friends and family.
- Use percentages: Rather than promote that tickets that cost 40 are now discounted by10, promote a 25 percent discount in prices. It sounds much bigger.

While numbers are exact, our brains think of pricing in a different way. Often the visitor is looking for an excuse to spend the money to buy the ticket. These ideas give the visitor permission to purchase because it's such a good deal (Nielson 2019)!

Task: Can I use some of these ideas in my ticket pricing strategy?

Event Plan: Use the information from this chapter to complete the first section of the event plan outline at the end of the book.

References

Modern Tribe. 2019. "Event Planning: Defining Event Goals and Objectives." *The Event Calendar*. December 1, 2019. https://theeventscalendar.com/blog/event-management/def ining-event-goals-and-objectives/. Accessed November 4, 2020.

Nielson, Frederick. 2019. "How to Price Tickets for an Event to Sell Out (in a Good Way)." *Billetto*. June 21, 2019. https://billetto.co.uk/blog/how-to-price-tickets-for-event/. Accessed November 14, 2020.

Quell, Molly. 2020. "EU Magistrate Pushes Back on Cashless Payment Rules." *Court House News*. September 29, 2020. https://www.courthousenews.com/eu-magistrate-pushes-bac k-on-cashless-payment-rules/. Accessed October 27, 2020.

Sandeep, Heda, Stephen Mewborn, and Stephen Caine. 2017. "How Customers Perceive a Price is as Important as the Price Itself." *Harvard Business Journal*. https://hbr.org /2017/01/how-customers-perceive-a-price-is-as-important-as-the-price-itself. Accessed December 12, 2020.

Sawyer, Katie. 2019. "Event Budgeting: How to Master Your Event Budget." *Eventbright Blog*. February 7, 2019. https://www.eventbrite.com/blog/event-budget-guide-ds00/. Accessed October 29, 2020.

Smith, Sarah. 2019. "6 Pricing Strategies for Your Next Event." *Eventbrite Blog Australia*. March 22, 2019. https://www.eventbrite.com.au/blog/pricing-strategies-next-event-ds00/ . Accessed November 22, 2020.

Stecker, Amaia. 2019. "5 Steps to Planning an Engaging Multiday Event." *Connect*. November 18, 2019. http://www.connectmeetings.com/association/features/5-steps-to-pl anning-an-engaging-multiday-event. Accessed August 4, 2020.

Woodruff, Jim. 2019. "What is Variance Analysis?" *Small Business Chronicle*. January 25, 2019. https://smallbusiness.chron.com/budget-variance-analysis-60250.html. Accessed August 7, 2020.

Chapter 7

Creating the event experience

Abstract

Part of any event experience is where it takes place. The venue might range from a traditional hotel meeting room to a public park. Visitors now desire events held at nontraditional venues such as museums, barns and wineries. Such places welcome events as a source of revenue. The venue for walking and bus tours is the route, which must be carefully planned for interest and accessibility. To attract visitors the event must be packaged with the needed lodging and eating establishments. Besides the core event, there need to be opportunities for visitor interaction and participation. It also must be packaged with entertainment for which contracts must be prepared. Walking tours should allow visitors to meet and interact with local residents. Activities and lessons should be part of the event. If food and beverages are provided, they should be chosen not only to be acceptable to the visitors but also to build on the theme of the event. This is part of the process of branding the event as a complete visitor experience.

Venues and routes

Venue is a broad term used for any type of building or outdoor area where tourism events take place. Events might take place in a building specifically designed for the purpose or a building designed for another purpose. For events such as tours, the venue will involve several different settings as it moves from place to place along the route. Because an event can be a package of several activities, it might involve finding and preparing several event venues or routes.

Venues are often described as traditional versus untraditional. Using the word "traditional" to describe a venue is unfortunate as it implies "boring." It can then be assumed that any untraditional venue will be exciting. This is not the distinction that should be made. Both can be boring or exciting depending on the creativity of those designing the event.

Traditional venues

When the event planners think of traditional venues, they may first think of hotel ballrooms and convention centers. The features that distinguished traditional venues are that they were purpose-built, neutral in design, and climate controlled. Because they were designed and built as event venues they will have a layout that will work for various types of events. They are often flexible, with the space capable of being enlarged if needed or having additional rooms added. Because some type of food and drink are needed at events, such venues will also have either kitchens or catering spaces available. Taken into consideration when the spaces were designed will be a way for tables and seating be set up and doors for delivery trucks to park near. All this makes the event easier to arrange and manage.

Another feature of traditional spaces is that they are neutral in design. While attractive, the design is kept without a theme so that events can be designed to incorporate their own theme. A hotel ballroom can be designed to host any type of event through decorations on the walls, hanging banners, table settings, flowers and music. Even aromas can be added. When using a traditional venue there is no need to find a place that fits the theme of the event. Being climate-controlled is another advantage of traditional spaces. While some nontraditional spaces are also climate-controlled, event managers using a traditional space don't need to worry about heat, cold, snow or rain.

Nontraditional venues

Nontraditional venues are spaces that were designed for other purposes than events. Because of this, they bring additional planning challenges. Nontraditional spaces that can be used include museums, tourism attractions, farms, fields, ships, wineries, airline hangers and caves. Any spot where the number of expected visitors can comfortably fit, and which meets the theme, can be used for an event. The reason there is a trend toward nontraditional spaces is that people want an event that is unique and memorable (Event 2018). Life is now more informal, so events are also.

Managers of nontraditional spaces are interested in hosting events as they are an additional source of revenue. However, one of the challenges is that the managers of the nontraditional venue will not be as skilled in hosting events. They may provide the space but nothing else. This means the event manager must arrange for the tables, seating and any technological equipment that will be needed. Second, depending on the venue, there may be little space for food preparation or even working space for a caterer.

An advantage of nontraditional venues is that the fee may be lower. Because the fee from event rentals is secondary to the major source of revenue, nontraditional venues can often offer a lower fee. This means that the event may need to be held outside of their normal business hours. For example, a planetarium that is open to the public during the day will only be able to host events in the evening. Because they are unique spaces, chosen because they express the desired theme, they may need less decoration.

If the nontraditional event space is outdoors, such as a field, patio or garden, weather will be a factor. The event will be planned for a time of year when the climate will be attractive but bad weather can happen any time of year. Sometimes it is possible to have a second date arranged for the event if the first is not acceptable, but for a public event this is rarely the case. Instead, there must be a contingency plan. This might involve a secondary nearby indoor space that can be used. Another idea is to have arranged a backup plan for rental of a tent or some other type of covering in case of bad weather. If the weather is dangerously bad, then the event may need to cancelled.

Venue advantages

- Traditional: Neutral design, climate-controlled, flexible spaces.
- Nontraditional: Themed, informal, less costly.

Tour routes

The venue for a tour is a complicated issue as it involves a starting place, route and ending place. If a vehicle is to be used to transport visitors on the tour, then the vehicle is also part of the venue. For a walking tour, one of the first considerations is time, distance and route length. These will depend on the age and interest level of visitors being targeted (Cook 2018). Tours should be of an appropriate length for visitors who may have difficulty walking for a long period of time. This may be due to age, but may also be due to disability. Long tours would also be of less interest to those not passionate about a subject. To meet the needs of both groups, separate tour routes might be developed: a short tour that only covers the major highlights and a more in-depth tour for those interested in detailed knowledge. Terrain along the route is also a consideration as steep hills, uneven cobblestones, and stairs may be a problem for some. Walking tours work best where the sites of interest are close together.

For tours covering longer distances, the visitors will need to be transported. The type of vehicle chosen should fit the theme of the tour. A generic rented bus will distract from the theme and even prevent bookings occurring. A historic vehicle or one that has signage in keeping with the theme is needed. The vehicle is part of the experience, not an afterthought. An interesting starting and ending point for the tours should be carefully chosen for the same reason. The meeting place where the tour starts is like the cover of a book. Unless it is interesting, the book will not be read and the tour will not be booked. The starting and ending points should also be convenient, with nearby public transportation or parking.

Tour route development considerations

- Starting and ending: Convenient locations for access.
- Transportation choice: Ease of walking or themed transport.
- Route layout: Appropriate content.
- Tour leader: Informative and entertaining.

Developing the event package

Packaging for a physical product can be thought of as merely the container that is used to protect it from damage or tampering on its way from production into the final hands of the consumer. However, besides offering protection, packaging is also used to communicate the benefits of the product. For example, if a souvenir is something that is used to beautify a home, the packaging would also be beautiful so as to communicate the benefit. A package can also be used to communicate the mission of the organization. For example, if part of the values of the organization is environmental awareness, the product can be packaged using recycled material (Lewis 2019). An organization's ethics are now considered part of the value that is received from a product.

There is also a need to package an event to communicate benefits and mission even though it is an event that offers intangible benefits such as excitement, local culture, a sense of history, or architectural beauty. Packaging of an event involves bundling the event's main attraction with other tourism products and services that become part or the brand. Branding involves creating a slogan and logo that will place the image of the event in the mind of the potential visitor along with the benefits the event will provide.

Meeting all visitor needs

The first decision that a potential visitor must make is what event to attend among the many available. If the visitor decides the event is of interest, it might be thought that marketing had been successful. Now it is understood that visitors are looking for a package of experiences, and unless this is available, they won't decide to attend. They will research the benefits offered by the event but also what other types of activities it offers. They will then want to know what else they can do while at the destination besides attending the event. This complete event package would also include meeting the need for somewhere to stay. The potential visitor would then research if there were interesting places to eat. Designing an event that offers a solution to all of these needs is the challenge faced by the organization.

When analyzing the type of event that the community can offer, the organization may discover that the proposed core event offers the features and benefits desired by only a small group of visitors. Unfortunately, attracting only these visitors may be insufficient to produce sufficient revenue. In this case, the product analysis that was conducted can then be used to adapt the event by determining what additional features the city is missing that are desired by a larger segment of potential visitors. Those responsible for developing the plan for the event can then work with the business community to add these features and benefits to develop a complete package.

For example, a city may already attract a small number of older tourists that attend a garden show event at a location known for its beautiful parks and gardens. Because the city needs to attract more visitors, they may decide to promote the event as a destination for families. To attract families, the organization would need to add activities that parents and children can enjoy together such as planting seedlings they can then take home. In addition, the organization will need to ensure that at least some of its lodging and eating establishments welcome children and pets. By doing so, the features the event already has to offer are enhanced and then can be promoted to a larger segment of visitors.

It may not be possible to change an event so that it provides a completely different experience. For example, if a community holds an event that is attractive to older tourists because of its many parks and gardens but has little active nightlife, attempting to target an entirely new segment of young people would be difficult.

Sometimes there may be what are called market failures in the economy. This is where there isn't a business that is interested in providing what is necessary to enhance the event. A lake, river or coast that can be enjoyed by visitors may be located close to the venue for an event. However, if there is no business that offers rentals for lifejackets, beach chairs or paddle boards, the organization may decide to do so during the period of the event. If there are trails, nearby bike rental could be offered if there is no business that does so.

Adding entertainment

Entertainment in some form will be part of the event package. It may be as simple as providing background music or it may be the focus of the event. Entertainment should be added any time there is a situation where visitors must wait, such as at the ticket booth (Murray 2018). The first step in planning and scheduling of entertainment will be research to find appropriate performers. One method is to simply ask friends if they know of anyone who might be available. Even if this method is going to be used, there still should be a procedure in place to ensure that the choice will be the best for a specific event.

The event organizers should see the performer in action, either live or on video. Most performers have websites or social media sites where they post video clips of past performances. These should be reviewed to assess the quality of the performance. Second, they need to be reviewed to ensure that the performance will not only be attractive to the visitors but also acceptable. It may be that the content is not age appropriate, may be offensive to some groups or politically unacceptable. As people can be quick to take offense, this is a critical part of the process. Even if the video clips seem to show that the performer will be a perfect fit, references should still be checked. Most performers will be happy to share the names of recent bookings for review purposes. It is best not to rely only on online reviews as it is unknown who has done the posting.

If the performer is acceptable and available the next step is to negotiate the contract. Part of this process is to learn their equipment and space needs. Even if they are providing all their own equipment such as instruments and microphones, it will be necessary to ascertain if the space and electrical capacity they need can be provided. If the performance is to be outside, the level of amplification needed should be verified. Finally, an outline of what will be performed and the length of the performance should be put in writing. There will be a fee that needs to be paid. It is critical to understand if any additional fees are expected, such as for transportation, lodging or food.

Hiring entertainment

- Research appropriate performers.
- Watch performance.
- Investigate content.
- Check reviews and references.
- Negotiate contract.

Visitor participation

Potential visitors are attracted to the main focus or core of the event. They will then want to know what other activities they can enjoy during the event. Scheduling planned activities is a way for visitors to enjoy, learn and interact with their fellow travelers. It is activities that engage the visitor that can provide a competitive advantage over other events. A quick computer search will find numerous events of every type. There is no shortage of music, theatre or dance festivals. There are also plenty of sporting events, historical commemorations and cultural festivals. As people are no longer interested in only being passive observers, choosing an event to attend is motivated by what type of other activities are available for participation.

The activities that are available should allow visitors to interact with each other. They are also an excellent means for visitors to interact with local community members. As much as possible activities should utilize local facilities and be run by local residents. Bringing in experts from outside the community might increase the level of skill but not provide the authentic experience that is desired by visitors.

Besides an opportunity to socialize, activities can provide an opportunity for physical activity. If the main event involves watching sports, activities should be planned that allow visitors to also participate, whatever their skill level. Some people are interested in learning. They will be motivated to attend workshops that involve active learning. If the main event involves local culture, activities on local foods and crafts can be planned. In the past there might have been scheduled lectures or talks about the theme of the event. Because people can easily find such information online, they will want an activity that involves participation rather than just passive listening. For example, they will want to prepare local food and try local crafts, not just be able to view them.

There may already be many activities available in the community that would be of interest to visitors. What is needed is to select ones that meet the theme of the event. These are the activities that will be promoted as part of the event package.

Event participation ideas

- Entertainment: Dance, instrumental singing, theatrical, readings.
- Tours: Historical, ethnic, food, alcohol.
- Activities: Making art, planting gardens, hiking.
- Lessons: Music, performance, crafts, cooking.

Creating tours

A tour might be the focus of the event. More commonly, tours are offered in addition to the main event. This might be a tour of an historic building, a neighborhood or a wilderness area. One of the first issues to consider is the demographics of the visitors for which the tour is intended. The distance should be of the correct length. Even people who have no physical limitations may find walking a distance difficult as they may not do so regularly. Also to be taken into consideration is the terrain. If there are hills that must be climbed, then the distance will need be to be shorter. If possible, it is best to avoid uneven surfaces as visitors intent on listening and watching could end up tripping. The length of the tour must match the interest level of the audience. Those planning the tour may find every bit of local or historic information exciting, while the visitors may enjoy a shortened version. Since taking and sharing photos is such an integral part of the visitor experience, the route should be planned with photo opportunities in mind.

Once the route is laid out, research on the tour content must be conducted. Those in charge of developing the tour should not simply rely on what they already know. All the information provided should be accurate. In any community, stories develop that, while interesting, are not based on facts. It is not critical to include every date someone was born or died or when a building was built. What is of interest is how what has happened in the past relates to the visitors on the tour today. They want interesting local information about real people not just historical figures.

The tour guide is the key to success of any tour. The person chosen to lead the tour needs to be well-spoken so they are easy to understand. Of course they should be knowledgeable on the content they are sharing. They also need excellent interpersonal skills. Not every visitor on the tour may be well-mannered and it is the tour leader's responsibility to ensure the enjoyment of the group. Most importantly, they need to be passionate. If *they* do not find what they are sharing of interest, then neither will the visitors.

While it might be tempting to only include well-known sites and historical figures on a tour, people can easily find this type of information online. What should be included are local stories that are unique to the community and not well known. Every tour will be different, but an example would be including small oases of nature in urban settings such as parks, courtyards and even private gardens. The stories of how these have been developed will be of interest. Community gathering places such as barbershops, diners and bars all can be the site of stories that relate to the event theme. Unusual stores can be used as focal points of tours and can add additional revenue to the businesses if visitors return to purchase. Any place that has to do with food will be of interest. This could be restaurants but also ethnic food stores, local markets and bakeries. Artist studios where visitors can watch people at work and also buy could be the focus of a tour. Visitors also love stories of the supernatural. While not necessarily true, these stories can be an entertaining way to share real local history.

It will be easier to market a tour with a theme beyond simply the history of the area. For example, if the community is a mix of interesting ethnic groups, then the tour could highlight not just the history but also the food, architecture or drinks unique to each. While guests are enjoying samples of these products at different stops, they will also learn more about the community and people. The tours should include famous sites, but also lesser-known sites that visitors would not discover on their own, which is the reason they are taking the tour. Meeting and hearing from locals on the tour is as important as having a knowledgeable local guide (Staford 2017).

While the sites may be fascinating, beautiful or both, it is the tour leader that will make the tour a success. People can follow a map on their own to see sites. What they want is the personal stories of the people behind the sites. The tour leader needs to be someone who is excited about sharing information beyond just dates and names. Some interactivity should be included in the tour rather than having visitors only listening. This could certainly be enjoying the taste of food or drink. It might also involve touch, such as having visitors try a local craft or handle old machinery. Movement might also be involved where the visitors try dance steps demonstrated by a local resident. These do not need to be at every stop on the tour, but taste, touch or movement should be included in the tour at some point.

Finally, visitors should have a way to return to the places of interest. A map can be provided that outlines the route and stops. This can be a physical map, but it is easiest if it is posted online. Another idea is to create a phone app that can be used by visitors that do not have time to participate in an organized tour (Villano 2017). There are now free platforms that can be used to develop such tours. These can then be either sold or access can be provided as part of a ticket package.

Activity ideas

The range of ideas for activities is almost endless. The decision on what should be included depends on whether it can be themed with the event. A workshop on bird watching will not be of interest to visitors attending a heavy metal music festival. It will also depend on having someone local who has both the skill and the personality to run the activity.

Activities can be related to sports, art, cultural, outdoors and performance. Sports-related activities might include competitions, photo opportunities with local sports personalities and tours of sports facilities. Related to art could be museum tours, walking tours of outside murals, and visiting local artist studios. They can be made even more participatory by having art lessons in various types of media. Outdoor activities can be organized hikes, jeep tours and garden tours. Each of these can be then enhanced. Hikers can be taught about the local plant life while visitors on jeep tours could learn more about the geological formation of the area. Garden tours could allow visitors to take cuttings to bring home to plant.

The opportunities involving food and beverage are almost endless. Cooking lessons and tasting locally produced alcohol are popular. To enhance them, learning about the culture while enjoying the products can be added.

Lessons

A lesson differs from an activity in that is more structured, with an expected learning outcome. This does not mean that it cannot be fun at any level of expertise. Beginning lessons can be offered to visitors who just want to experience what it would be like to try a new skill. Advanced lessons can be offered if there is visitor interest and someone with the expertise to teach.

Lessons are promoted to the visitors as a chance to learn and experience a skill for which they do not have the time or access to at home. It is easy to think of lessons being offered in the performance arts of music, singing and dance. In addition, lessons in the visual arts of painting, drawing, sculpture and photography can also be offered to visitors. Traditional craft areas are also of interest to visitors, including everything from weaving to blacksmithing. Other crafts might be jewelry making, quilting and bee keeping. What is critical is that what is provided is not a list of every possible activity but a curated list of what activities fit the theme of the event.

Theming food and beverage

There will always be a need for some type of refreshment at any event. Even with a simple walking tour, bottles of water should be made available as it demonstrates a concern for the visitor's comfort. For a larger event, catering will be needed. The type and quality of the food provided will greatly influence the visitor's event experience. For a small event, catering purchased from a local restaurant may be all that is needed. For larger events, a professional catering company may be required.

Food and beverage options

- Food: Food trucks, catering, vendors, sit-down meal, food stations.
- Beverage: Beer and wine, spirts, non-alcoholic, coffee and tea.

Catering

Some venues will have an already existing arrangement to handle the refreshment needs for events. They may either use their own staff or they may require anyone using the venue to use a specific vendor. Even if the tourism organization believes there is a less expensive option, there are advantages to using the venue staff or catering company. The staff or catering company have already been screened for quality. The venue would not want to use a company that would damage their reputation. The other advantage is that the catering company will be already familiar with the food preparation and serving capacity of the venue. Different menu items will require different types of cooking facilities and preparation areas. An outside company may not be aware of these restrictions, resulting in problems with food preparation when the event is occurring.

If the event organizers are planning on hiring their own catering company, there are a number of considerations. First would be if the company can handle the size of the event. If the event is small, the caterer may not be interested in the contract. The caterer might feel it was not financially feasible to enter into an agreement. The other issue is whether the catering company can handle the size of a large event as they may not have the staff or cooking facility to do so. The location is also a consideration. Having a caterer that is located far from the venue can create problems with logistical issues such as weather and traffic. Another issue is flexibility. A catering company with a good reputation may be scheduled out many months in advance. The tourism organization may not know the size the event and the amount of food needed until shortly before the event takes place. A consideration when deciding on a company is the cutoff date for when the final order must be placed and what will be the effect on costs of any last-minute changes to the numbers. Verifying that the caterer has all the necessary licenses and insurances is also critical.

While the caterer may have wonderful marketing material, checking online reviews and getting references from past customers is critical. These should be reviewed not just as to whether they are positive or negative but if there are problems highlighted that are of concern to the organization as there will always be some negative postings. Because people have individual preferences by which they define quality, the organization should request that a tasting be arranged. Most caterers will be happy to provide samples of what they prepare.

The next step would be to review pricing, which can vary for the same event depending on what is going to be served. The organization must decide how important food is to the event. If the event is promoted as including a gourmet dinner then more expensive menu items will be expected. Choosing a company to provide food for a festival where visitors just want to grab something to eat can result in a simpler, less expensive choice. The catering company may charge additional fees, such as mileage and set-up fees that may be added to the contract. The organization must be clear that they are aware of all fees before the contract is signed.

Theming food to the event

Without making drastic changes to the menu, food can be themed to any event (Luppino-Esposito nd). Most meals will have some type of bread and desert and both of these can be used to easily reflect the culture of an event. If the event is themed around the environment, using only local vendors or food trucks can fit with the event mission and values. An event that is focused on history can also have unique food offerings. Having candy or other treats that were common during the time period can help visitors experience the past. The actual flavors might need to be adjusted to fit present tastes as there is no benefit to theming food that no one will enjoy eating.

No matter what the theme, the dietary restrictions of visitors should be considered. These are numerous and can be because of religion, health or environmental concerns. There could be religious prohibitions on eating certain types of foods. The event might also be taking place when a religion is observing periods of fasting. Some people for religious reasons, and some for personal, abstain from drinking types of alcohol or caffeinated drinks. Vegetarians and vegans will also require consideration when planning the menu. Other issues such as common allergies to foods should be considered. If certain ingredients cannot be avoided, then the food contents should be labeled.

Theming alcohol to the event

Just as with catering companies, the venue chosen for the event may have the capacity to provide and serve alcohol or have an existing arrangement with a company to provide both drinks and bartending services. If not, there are several issues that must be considered when planning for a bar at an event. The first issue is whether the visitor or the organization is paying for the drinks. At some high-priced events, it may be expected that at least some alcohol is provided, with additional drinks being purchased by the visitor. A second issue is what type of alcohol will be served, which could be only beer and wine, or it may include stronger-proof spirits.

The alcohol served can also be themed to the type of event: for example, tropical drinks at a summer outdoor event or just locally brewed beer at an event focused on sports. The price of alcohol will vary depending on the cost of the brand. Some visitor segments will not care about brand name and any drink will be acceptable. A different segment may only be pleased if high-quality brands are served.

Besides the alcohol, other items will include mixers and non-alcoholic drinks for non-drinkers. Embellishments such as fruit slices will also be needed. If a full service bartending company is chosen they will provide these items and also the ice and glassware. They may even be able to provide their own bar. The price for the service will vary greatly depending on what types and the number of drinks that will be provided. A consideration is that the interaction of the bartending staff with the visitors is part of the ambience of the event. While a bartender should be aware of any individuals who have already consumed enough drinks, they should be denied additional drinks with professionalism and courtesy.

While both catering and bartending companies must follow safety guidelines, there are additional requirements for bartenders. These individuals may require licensing from the government. This licensing may involve training on how to stop underage drinking and also to handle signs of intoxication. Because of the liability issues involved in serving alcohol, only appropriately licensed or trained individuals should be used to serve drinks. However, the organization can save money by providing all the alcohol and necessary equipment.

When serving alcohol at an event it is critical that all requirements and restrictions be followed. These will vary by country and also by local laws and regulations. There will be age restrictions on who can legally serve alcohol. There may also be requirements that someone serving alcohol be licensed to do so. The training usually requires knowledge of how to limit intoxication. There will also be laws on the age people can legally drink. In some areas this age may vary by type of alcohol. Extra insurance may be needed to cover liability. Everyone involved in the event should be aware that someone who over-consumes alcohol can cause a disruption that will negatively affect the enjoyment of other guests. The event organizers may also be legally liable if someone who becomes intoxicated at the event is involved in an automobile accident after they leave.

Of course, alcohol does not need to be served. This may be a budget choice made by the organization. It might also result from cultural considerations. In this case, refreshments still need to be served. A beverage station that offers different types of sodas, teas and waters can be made festive using fancy glassware and exotic flavors. Such an arrangement is especially needed at events targeted at families.

Discussion questions

1. What is the advantage of holding an event in a traditional venue?
2. Why are visitors interested in attending events in nontraditional venues?
3. What factors should be considered when deciding on the route for a walking tour?
4. Why must the core event be packaged with other activities?
5. How should entertainment be chosen for an event?
6. Why are contracts essential when booking entertainment or speakers?
7. How can activities, lessons or tours be themed to motivate attendance?
8. How can food and beverage be used to enhance the event?
9. Why does extra care need to be taken when serving alcohol?

Case

Nontraditional venue challenges

It seems that everyone who is going to an event wants to get out of the hotel room and into some place exciting. Maybe it's because they want a new experience or perhaps because it will be more informal. Whatever the reason, the use of such places as wineries, museums, public parks, warehouses, and even airplane hangars, is growing. The advantage for the organization planning the event is that it will not only attract visitors but also create buzz on social media. Sometimes it can even be cheaper than renting a traditional space. However, there are challenges that need to be considered.

*   Accessibility: Such places may have physical barriers that will interfere with the enjoyment of visitors with disabilities – plan ahead with portable ramps.
*   Power: While they may have power, it may not be enough for the equipment that will be needed for the planned entertainment – bring a generator.
*   WIFI: Some buildings will interfere with Internet connections of visitors and not have available connectivity to compensate – have a hot spot.

- Permitting: Just because the venue is interested in hosting, doesn't mean that it can be legally used to host a crowd – check with the city.
- Transportation: Getting people to the event, having parking and getting people back can be a problem if the venue was not designed with a crowd in mind – use coaches or ride share (Echelon 2020).

Task: What nontraditional venue might you use and how will you meet the challenges?

Case

You will need help

Visitors will expect lots of activities at your event. This presents a problem. They also want to interact with the local community. This presents a solution. Instead of hiring extra staff, the event can make use of local volunteers. Why would someone volunteer? You can offer free admission, not just to them, but also their family members. Where can you find these volunteers? You can contact community groups as volunteering can be more fun when done together. Many communities also have websites that match volunteers to organizations. Finding volunteers is only the first step. To make effective use of them, follow these steps:

- Ask their interests and skills to match them to the right task they can do and enjoy.
- Have an orientation with free food for everyone that explains the purpose of the event.
- Share a code of conduct to ensure that everyone has a positive experience.
- Provide any needed training such as with ticketing technology before the event.
- At the event, make sure all the volunteers know who to contact in case they need help.
- Be sure and thank them after the event and they may be willing to help again next year (Torres 2017).

Task: Put together a plan for using volunteers at event activities.

Event plan: Use the information from this chapter to complete the first section of the event plan outline at the end of the book.

References

Cook, Ron. 2018. "Creating Engaging Tours." *Main Street America*. October 3, 2018. https ://www.mainstreet.org/blogs/national-main-street-center/2018/10/03/creating-engaging-walking-tours. Accessed November 5, 2020.

Echelon Design. 2020. "The Rise of the Nontraditional Venue." *Echelon Design*. March 2, 2020. https://echelondesign.com/2020/03/02/the-rise-of-the-destination-meeting/. Accessed October 20, 2020.

Event Leadership Institute. 2018. "Benefits of Untraditional Event Venues." *Event Leadership Institute*. May 15, 2018. https://eventleadershipinstitute.com/benefits-untraditional-event-venues/ Accessed November 4, 2020.

Lewis, Colin. 2019. "Ethics Are Central to Consumers New Definition of Value." *Marketing Week*. June 13, 2019. https://www.marketingweek.com/colin-lewis-new-definition-of-value/. Accessed December 10, 2020.

Luppino-Esposito, Amanda. n.d. "The True Role of Food and Beverage in Marketing Events." *Social Tables*. https://www.socialtables.com/blog/catering/role-food-and-beverage/. Accessed December 12, 2020.

Murray, Katie. 2018. "10 Tips to Keep Your Attendees Entertained (and Happy!)" *SpinGo*. August 20, 2018. https://www.spingo.com/blog/post/10-tips-to-keep-your-attendees-entertained-and-happy. Accessed December 15, 2020.

Staford, Anna. 2017. "Why Spending Time with Locals Should Be in Your Travel To-Do List." *Globelink*. April 4, 2017. https://www.globelink.co.uk/articles/travel-information/why-spending-time-with-locals.html. Accessed September 6, 2020.

Torres, Alyssa. 2017. "All You Need to Know to Recruit, Train and Manage Event Volunteers." *EventBright Blog*. September 28, 2017. https://www.eventbrite.com/blog/event-volunteers-ds00/. Accessed July 14, 2020.

Villano, Matt. 2017. "Create Your Own Walking Tour with This App." *AFAR*. August 22, 2017. https://www.afar.com/magazine/create-your-own-walking-tour-with-this-app. Accessed October 2, 2020.

Chapter 8

Managing the event

Abstract

Management is needed to ensure that the day of the event is a success. Security needs to be provided at events to handle any disruptions caused by visitors. Security is also needed in the case of accidents and emergencies. Visitors will expect events to minimize the effect they have on the environment. This includes the materials that are used and also recycling and waste management. While visitors are interested in learning about other cultures, event organizers need to ensure that any representation of other cultures is respectful and accurate. There are creative aspects of events including deciding on the theme. There are also management responsibilities that include coordinating all event logistical details. Management of the day of the event requires the ability to prioritize and deal with any crisis. Event management takes organizational and interpersonal skills. A detailed agenda will be needed of all tasks along with completion dates and the name of the person responsible. Using an electronic template will assist in managing all details so the event runs smoothly. Recruiting qualified employees for the event can be done through local sources. There should be a standard policy used for interviewing and hiring. If independent contractors are used, they will also need to be supervised.

Addressing security, social and health concerns

When planning tourism events visitor concerns on security, sustainability, cultural respect and health issues must be considered. Not every visitor will be concerned with all of these issues but they must be addressed for those who are. Addressing these concerns will not attract visitors uninterested in the event content. Not addressing these concerns will cause some visitors to not attend an event they would otherwise have attended.

Security

Ensuring everyone has a safe and enjoyable event without disruption is the goal of security. For a small-scale event security can be handled by the organization. For any larger event, security staff should be hired. Although this is an added expense, the reputation of the event will be damaged if it is disrupted by unruly people or there is an emergency that staff are unable to handle.

Another security issue is crisis management. Security should be prepared for events that are fortunately rare, but can happen (Bishop 2020). This would include a natural disaster and terrorism or other crime. It would also include weather events such as storms. Handling the crowd so that it safely evacuates the site or helping someone with an injury or medical issue is beyond the abilities of tourism staff and volunteers. Security staff will have given thought before the event to a safe exit procedure, equipment needed and staff training.

Before hiring a security company, it should be confirmed that they have all necessary licenses and permits required by the local government. Security staff should also have training and certification in basic first aid. In addition, the company being considered should have experience at similar events. Security companies that routinely work large rock concerts may not be suitable for working a family event. Before hiring, references should be checked to ensure that the security staff have suitable customer service skills. While trained to handle problems, they should also be friendly and helpful when approached with routine requests.

Before the day of the event, the security company or event organizers should contact local police and ambulance services to let them know of the event they will be working. This way, if any additional services are needed, coordination will be easy. A walkthrough of the venue should be held to decide on security checkpoints. Such a checkpoint may be needed at the entrance to enforce any restrictions on what can be brought on site. Additional security staff may be needed where alcohol is being served to assist in dealing with visitors who may have drunk a little too much. If a very popular entertainer is performing, security will be needed to handle over-excited fans.

Security staff are trained to patrol the event venue to stop problems before they occur. They ensure a positive experience for visitors as they are trained in spotting trouble before it can be noticed by others. They will also be present to assist if there is a problem with a specific guest or with the need to vacate the premises quickly due to an emergency. Another safety issue is to ensure that the event does not become overcrowded as the permit may place a limit on the number of visitors allowed in the venue. Lastly, security is in charge of preventing theft of money, supplies or equipment.

Sustainability

Travelers know that visiting another country or even the next town has an effect on the environment. This would include everything from carbon generated by aircraft to single-use product dispensers made of plastic placed in hotel bathrooms. A study found that travelers are concerned about the environmental effects of traveling. They are also aware that tourism, if handled with environmental sustainability in mind, can have a positive effect on communities (Stone 2019).

An event that addresses the issue of sustainability will try to increase the enjoyment of the event for visitors while minimizing the use of resources. The public is interested in minimizing the amount of waste that is produced, so materials used should be able to be reused or else recycled. This might not always be possible. For example, because of health regulations it may be necessary to use disposable dishes when serving food at an event without the necessary sanitation equipment. Even so the choice of materials when serving food should focus on dishes and cutlery that can be easily recycled and this information should be posted online and at the venue.

Recycling bins are now standard at most events. Visitors may become unhappy if they are not available and believe the organization does not care about the environment. To minimize trash, instead of handing out paper programs or events, large posters of events can be used where visitors can take a photo on their phone and use it for reference. Electronic ticketing rather than paper tickets is another example of minimizing waste.

Appropriate representation of culture

Most visitors have a sincere interest in learning about other cultures. This interest can be one of the primary motives for attending an event. Even smaller communities may have people from a different cultural background that nearby visitors will find of interest. When using cultural artefacts or practices as part of an event, it is critical to do so appropriately.

There is a difference between cultural appropriation and cultural appreciation (Ngata 2019). Cultural appropriation is when items such as ceremonial clothing are used without understanding their purpose. This can be offensive to the members of the cultural group that understands their ceremonial meaning. For example, having visitors pose for photos in robes that have a religious significance can be offensive. Likewise performing a dance that is only used in traditional funeral ceremonies can be seen as wrong by members of the culture. The reason that many people of other cultures find this offensive is that they may have experienced oppression by other groups. Even if this is not true, their culture may have been dominated by the majority culture, leaving the group to feel invisible in their own country.

It is not that culture should not be shared; it is how it is done that matters. After all, meeting new people and learning from them is one of the reasons for travel. Learning about other cultures can also help a visitor understand their own culture by contrasting their own way of life with what they are experiencing. Cultural appreciation, rather than appropriation, is using artifacts and practices to learn and share rather simply mimic. To do so appropriately, a member of the culture being represented should be involved so they can demonstrate the correct use of the object. Visitors can learn while they enjoy seeing the use of the object, such as a musical instrument, being demonstrated.

Cultural immersion is when the visitor is involved in the cultural practice. Learning a local craft or how to cook an ethnic food that is from a different culture can be a means of both education and enjoyment. The lessons can be seen as an opportunity for others to gain appreciation of the talent needed to perform the task. People from the local culture can provide the best guidance as to what is acceptable and will not cause offense.

Health concerns

Traveling to improve health and wellbeing has always existed. It has become more popular with a double-digit percentage growth each year (Rubinstein 2020.) People visit spas, hot springs and mountain environments to become more physically fit and also live a healthier lifestyle when they return home.

While tourism and hospitality have always wanted to provide safe experiences to visitors, since the pandemic of 2020 there has been an increased vigilance on maintaining a healthy environment for visitors. People are now assuming that travel can be dangerous and want preventive measures taken. As a result, visitors who were previously unconcerned are now aware how travel can negatively affect their health. Information should be shared on how health concerns are being addressed through new cleaning protocols. Because visitors are now concerned with being in a crowded enclosed space that can facilitate the spread of disease, more outdoor events might be considered. The idea of enjoying an experience with a minimum need to touch possibly contaminated surfaces is resulting in more technology being used for ticket purchase and check-in to lodging and events.

Addressing common event issues

- Security: Handle staff, hire service, provide training.
- Sustainability: Trash reduction, recycling, local sourcing.
- Cultural: Accurate representation, connections with local communities.
- Health: Cleanliness, medical emergencies, sanitation.

Event management process

Tourism and hospital events need to be planned but also need to be managed. While everyone can be involved in the process of choosing the event theme, finding a venue and deciding on entertainment and activities, management has specialized responsibilities for which not everyone will be suited. Event planners have most input into the process in creating the overall theme of the event and the activities that will create the theme. Event managers have the responsibility of handling all the details before, during and after the event that make the event a reality. Both are needed and in a small organization the same people may play both roles (Collins 2020). Management tasks include the less exciting process of handling the details of contracts with entertainment and vendors. Other responsibilities include hiring and training any needed staff. Management is also responsible for ensuring that everything runs smoothly on the day of the event.

Logistical issues must be addressed, including getting the required licenses, permits and insurance. These issues are best handled by someone with management skills. Other management tasks that are common to any type of event include deciding on equipment needs, signage, sanitation and managing the process of ticket taking. Because an event can be anything from a multiple-day festival to a single historic walking tour, the event planning and management needs for each must be analyzed separately. What will be needed for every event no matter how large or small is a schedule of activities and responsibilities for the day of the event. The development and implementation of this schedule is a management responsibility.

While event planning takes a high level of creative skill, the management side of the event requires a different skill set. Handling management responsibilities requires organizational ability. Managers must have the ability to keep in mind how all the components of the event must be coordinated. To ensure that every task is completed when resources are limited, a manager needs the ability to prioritize. As management is responsible for ensuring the event runs smoothly, the ability to problem-solve under pressure is also needed. It may be that with a small staff, everyone will be involved in all aspects of both planning and managing the event. In this case the staff must have strong interpersonal skills and the ability to work as a team.

Managing the event planning process

The design, marketing and management of events is a process. It starts with researching the idea for an event. This is when the objectives for the event are determined. The reason for holding the event can be to build awareness of the destination, to increase visitation of a particular target market or simply to increase revenue for businesses within the community. It could also be all three of these objectives. The development of the objectives will involve input from all the participants in the community. This would include tourism organizations, lodging establishments, business and even nonprofit organizations. A management responsibility is to ensure that the necessary meetings are held to gather this information. The planning meetings are essential as a means to build relationships and gain future cooperation.

Once the objectives are clear, the creative planning begins by deciding on a theme for the event. This theme will depend on two factors. First, it must authentically be tied to the identity of the location where the event will be held. People will not just be attending an event; they will be visiting a community. Second, the theme must be attractive to a specific visitor segment. This segment might be defined by demographics such as age or family stage. It also might be defined by lifestyle, such as adventurous or traditional. The event is the reason for the visit but there must be more benefits to attract visitors. This is why the event theme must be representative of a community as a whole. There will be disagreements on the event theme as different community members will represent different interests. Managers must ensure everyone is heard and help all stakeholders come to a final agreement on the event.

Initial planning steps overseen by management

- Assess the community for event ideas.
- Decide on the type of event.
- Determine the event theme and any additional needed services.
- Perform SWOT Analysis.
- Determine visitor segment(s) to target.

Once the objectives and themes are developed, the next stage in planning is developing the budget. This is a task that will require management skill to control costs. It is the reality of budget constraints that makes the development of a theme challenging. While creative individuals on the organizing team may have wonderful ideas, management must remind them of the reality of limited funds available for implementation of the idea. A decision will need to be made as which venue will be used for the event, whether a room, an entire building, an outside space or a route for a walking tour. The budget will determine what type of venue can be used, such as renting a lavish room or holding the event in a public park. It will also determine whether professional entertainment can be hired or if there will be a need to use local groups. Management needs to ensure that the costs can be covered by revenue.

Once the budget is set, the venue can be finalized. The planning process will then move to the decisions on entertainment and food. Many other decisions will be involved, such as technology and equipment requirements. If vendors are to be included, the decision as to what type needs to be addressed. This process will take significant management oversight. While making the right decision on theme will be what attracts visitors, managing the details of the event will determine if the event is successful once the visitors arrive.

The next step in the process is managing the implementation of all the event components. The coordination of an event is similar to building a house. A finished house requires multiple products, such as lumber, bricks, windows, and also people, such as carpenters, electricians, plumbers. All these materials and people must be on the work-site in a specific order as the windows can't be installed until the walls are built. When the owners of a new house enter through the door, all they see is their new home, without thought to how it was created. An event is similar; the management tasks of planning and coordination are hidden from view but are essential. The coordination will involve ensuring that everyone involved in the production of the event knows not only their responsibilities but also when they are to be completed. This type of work needs to be done by someone with an understanding of management.

Managing the timeline

It is best if planning for an event starts at least six months out. It is not unusual for the planning of a large event to start a year ahead. Early decisions that must be made include the theme, targeted visitor segment, venue and date. When all the activities and entertainment are decided, the equipment and personal needed on the day of the event are listed along with who will be responsible to ensure they are available. At this time, the options for food and beverage must be decided. Also decided upon will be the targeted vendors and sponsors. This information will also be listed with the names of those responsible.

Three months from the event, detailed planning can begin. Each of the categories above will have their own detailed list. For example, the list for venue would include the transportation arrangements to the site and the need for vendor parking. Set-up of decorations, stages and ticketing areas will now need to described in detail and assigned to those responsible. The need for any special arrangements for accessibility will be detailed. The final arrangements for any entertainment or speakers including contracts, travel arrangements and special equipment for needs will be listed. Details on food and beverage would include dates for sampling and final menu decisions.

The planning list should also include more mundane items such as the arrangements for toilet facilities for outdoor events and security, if needed. Production items that need to be considered on the planning list would be sound and audiovisual needs. For outdoor events electricity will need to be provided along with lighting for nighttime events. Events that have entertainment may also need a stage. Vendors may need tables and tents if they do not provide their own. All these details will be listed along with the date they need to be accomplished and the name of the person responsible.

The promotion of the event will have its own timeline. This will include such items as development of print material and creation of social media sites. The times when marketing content must be created and who will do the posting will be detailed. Finally, specific social media that are needed for the success of the event should be decided and listed. This might include such items as photo booths or Instagram walls. The need for Internet access also needs to be addressed. One month before the event, all the details in the above lists will need to be finalized. Of course, there will be many changes. This could result from new ideas that have been suggested or because of external changes such as an entertainer cancellation.

Developing the agenda

Finally, it will come to the day of the event. Here is where management skills are needed the most. To manage the event an agenda will be created that lists all of the activities that will take place during the event from start to finish. Next, a detailed timeline is developed as to when everything will take place. Finally, people must be assigned responsibility to ensure that the activities take place on time so that the event runs successfully. A detailed agenda will take a significant time to develop. There may be a temptation to simply assume everything will run smoothly, but this will rarely happen. Even with advance planning, some things will inevitably go wrong due to factors outside of the organization's control.

Assigning times

Creative individuals who work in tourism and hospitality often have a task-oriented relationship with time. This means that once excited about a task they will work until the task is completed, with little awareness of the time that is passing. Managing an event process needs a different approach. To keep on-task requires thinking of time as having a pre-existing structure that must be used efficiently. Sometimes it is thought that working intensively for long periods of time means that people are working hard. However, it may only mean that people are staying stuck on the same task.

Tracking the implementation of the event plan means that it will be necessary for managers to help other staff to structure their assigned tasks to keep within a time limit. The best way to do so is to have regular meetings reviewing where each task is in relation to where it should be on the timetable. Once this is done, the staff who are having trouble completing tasks should be encouraged to handle a small but difficult task and get it out of the way so they can move on to other tasks. For many people, the morning is the best time to accomplish the required tasks because a sense of success can result in the remaining tasks not seeming to be so difficult. After the first task is completed, the remainder of the day's tasks can be done.

Some creative staff may find this type of structure difficult when they are not inspired (Rue 2018). To help keep them on track, the tasks assigned should be of interest. As some staff work well independently when inspired but can become quickly bored and stop contributing to the effort, it is a management task to keep them on track.

Day-of-event management tasks

All the planning that has taken place will hopefully result in a successful event. However, many problems can still arise on event day for which management must be prepared. For large events, set up may start a day before or even earlier. For smaller events held in rented venues, it may only be possible to have access hours before the event.

Some of the immediate tasks involve the placement of signage so that visitors can find the access point. Signage should also be in place for toilet, smoking and coat-check areas. The entry way for ticket selling, or scanning, if none are sold on site, must be prepared with personnel in place. Any equipment and technology should be checked to see if it is in the correct location. Most importantly, it should be verified that everything is in working order. There should be no last-minute surprises such as microphones, Wi-Fi, or lighting that are not working just when the performance is to start. Management should also verify the arrival of entertainers and speakers. Packages of supplies for any activities should be checked for accuracy.

Staff and volunteers should be greeted and their responsibilities should be reviewed. Their hours should be clarified, along with any appropriate breaks. A comfortable area where staff can enjoy their breaks along with refreshments should be provided if possible.

Planning templates

Part of the process described above is developing a timeline that can be followed. Many project management templates can be found online that can be used for this purpose. The complexity of the timeline will depend on the complexity of the event. The more activities, vendors, entertainment, catering and lodging that is involved, the more detailed the timeline becomes. The use of a software template to track competition of tasks should be considered as it will save time and also help ensure staff responsiveness. There are many free software templates available that can also be run as apps on a smartphone. Some are generic while others are specific to a type of event and may not be appropriate.

A Gantt chart, which can be easily found online, is a generic template often used by organizations that can be customized for any purpose. It is a bar chart that can track the progress of many tasks simultaneously using a visual method that makes it easy to understand where the organization is in relation to deadlines for completion of the plan. The first step in using this method is to determine what will be the start and end dates for implementation of the entire event process. Then each task is listed, along with the time it will take to complete. Whether any task must be completed before another, or if some tasks must be completed simultaneously, should be determined. These tasks and times are then put into a chart.

One of the major advantages of using such a chart is that it explains visually all the tasks that need to be completed and their interrelationships. By doing so, it reduces the risk that a task will not be completed and caused to fail. This will help to explain to staff how others in the organization depend on their completion of assigned tasks. Another advantage is that if a task does take longer than was assigned, this information can be recorded, so a more accurate timeline can be developed for the next event. Lastly, if a task is not completed, there is a record of accountability that can be easily seen by everyone in the organization. Many individuals can more easily understand a visual representation than a written list. This method should keep individuals motivated to complete their assigned tasks.

Hiring event staff

It is a management task, when planning an event, to assign responsibility for tasks so that everything gets done. The challenge is assigning an appropriate task that matches the skills with the person charged with completion. One way to do so is to first think of skills in broad categories. Someone with interpersonal skills will need to confirm that each task is completed in a timely manner. They will also be responsible for any personnel issues such as underperformance or conflicts within the team. It is best someone with financial skills is responsible for budgeting and oversite. This person would not work in isolation but would be in charge of creating the budget for the event and then ensuring that costs are kept under control. Marketing also needs to have someone with specific skills in social media and marketing to design and implement a promotional message. The program for the event, including entertainment and activities, will involve the task of finding and hiring performers. The person put in charge of this component will also need to create activities that engage visitors. Finally, logistics and legal issues, including such components as transportation, sanitation, contracts and permits, will need to be handled by someone who enjoys working with details. If the staff organizing the event is small, these responsibilities will need to be shared.

Hiring staff process

Because new events may start small, all the responsibilities involved can be handled by current staff members. However, if the event is successful, the time will come when the decision will need to be made whether to hire additional staff members. While it might seem like an easy, and maybe even logical, next step, in fact it means that the person in charge of the event will now become a personnel manager. Taking on this role means new responsibilities, which include job analysis and the tasks associated with recruiting and hiring employees.

The first task when considering hiring an employee is to determine exactly what the employee will be doing each day while on the job. It is not enough to simply state that help is needed, as finding the right employee depends on understanding what skills are necessary to perform the required tasks. If tourism and hospitality staff believe they can no longer run the event on their own, they should consider what tasks they are currently doing that could be done by someone else. There are two types of tasks for which someone may need to be hired. The first are those that require a high level of specialized skill. The second are tasks that require a low level of skill, where it would be a waste of current staff time to not hire someone else to do the job.

A job analysis is a list of tasks that will be done by an employee. This task analysis will help to determine the days and number of hours that will need to be worked. It may be that a full-time employee is not needed. Even if only a part-time employee is needed, it must be determined what days and hours they will be required to be present. Once the task list is completed, it should be determined what skills, education and personality traits are required to do the job. With this information, a job description can be written. It is this job description that will be used to find applicants most likely to be successful once they are hired.

The new employee who joins the organization should believe in the mission of the organization and not just want a job. In addition, they should be excited about participating in the event. The new employee should not be thought of as simply as someone who is hired to do tasks, but instead as a partner in achieving a successful event. Many potential employees are looking for places to work where they feel they are making a difference and not just performing a job (Hodges 2017).

Recruiting qualified candidates

Hiring someone who is already known by someone within the organization can be an advantage. Not only will the organization have some knowledge of the potential employee but they may already be familiar with the culture of the organization. Therefore, spreading the word within the organization that a new employee is needed is the first step. Another idea is to approach university career offices and local job placement centers for qualified candidates. Current interns who are already familiar to the organization can be hired on a permanent basis. If necessary, the job can be advertised on a website. However, most employers wish to avoid this step, if possible, because of the time it takes to review and respond to all the applications, many of which will be from people who are not qualified for the position.

Interviewing and hiring candidates

While the recruitment process can be informal, the interview process needs to be more thoughtful and structured, as it is part of the legal process of hiring an employee. While the legal requirements will vary, normally the first step is to review applications. Even if the future employee is known to the organization, there should still be an application process that asks for education and employment history. If the application demonstrates the necessary skills and education, an interview can be scheduled.

Before the interview starts, the organization should prepare a list of questions. For fairness and comparability, each applicant should be asked the same questions, none of which should relate to the applicant's personal life, as such questions may be illegal. However, the interview is more than just a list of questions and answers. It is also about matching the applicant's values and personality with those of the organization. Each organization has a culture into which the new employee must fit. Staff planning and managing an event will work closely together under sometimes stressful conditions and therefore must be able to get along.

If the applicant performs well in the interview, there is one last step to be taken before the position is offered, which is to check references. Again, it is necessary to understand the applicable employment law regarding asking and verifying references. It needs to be done because it is not uncommon for applicants to either withhold information or outright lie about their qualifications. Letters of reference are not enough proof as they can be easily faked. The applicant needs to provide the name and number of a former employer or other professional referee, such as a professor. Some employers may feel uncomfortable verifying the statements made by applicants. However, it should be remembered that the organization's reputation and financial standing can be harmed by the actions of an employee.

Once the decision has been made to hire, the paperwork starts. First, the applications of unsuccessful applicants, along with notes explaining why they were not chosen, need to be retained. This is done for legal purposes, in case applicants decide they were not hired for discriminatory reasons. Second, the paperwork associated with hiring the successful candidate needs to be prepared. A formal contract may not be needed, but any new employee should be provided with the written job description, their work schedule and the pay amount.

Hiring independent contractors

A tourism organization may often need employees for a specific task rather than part-time employment. This might be for such tasks as tech support, marketing or design work. If the job can be done at the time and place of the employee's choosing, they are considered an independent contractor. These employees were often referred to as freelance labor in the past. This is not a new concept but increasingly common with the growth of the gig economy. What is new is that such employees may now be easily found and contracted through websites.

Having a contract for this type of work is particularly important as the work may be done remotely. This arrangement does not allow for easy review of the work in progress, leaving the organization vulnerable to poor-quality completed work (Lozano 2018). The contract should include a detailed description of the tasks to be performed. This should include all details on the final work product that is expected and should specify a date for its completion. Expectations for review of work in progress need to be written down to ensure that the final product is acceptable. Finally, the basis of payment, whether hourly or by project, should be explained in detail. Failure to document these expectations may leave the organization with substandard work, a higher-than-expected bill or, even worse, both.

Managing contracts

All entertainers, speakers or others who are going to be paid for their appearance at the event need to have a contract. When the person performing is known to the organization, it might be tempting to believe a contract is not necessary. However, conflicts on the quality of the work or the amount that is to be paid can arise. It is better to have a signed contract that is not needed than to later need a contract and not have one prepared.

Some details required for a contract are self-evident. The name of the organization responsible for hiring and their contact information should be included. The names and addresses of all performers should be included as this information may be needed for tax reporting. The type of entertainment should be described so that there are no last-minute surprises. Any restrictions on content should be included in the contract. For example, the contract might specify that certain topics are off-limits, such as the current political situation or that the entertainment be appropriate for children.

Of course, the price that will be paid, along with when payment will be made, should be included. It may be customary for a percentage of the total payment to be paid before the event, with the remainder after completion. This section should also include what will happen if either the performer or organization cancel the event or if unforeseen circumstances force the event to be cancelled.

Some of the other issues include copyright and photo releases. If the organization plans on using video of the performance on their social media sites, permission to do so should be granted in writing. The agreement should also include any additional payment due to the entertainer . It is common for a photo release to be granted so that images from the event can be used in future promotion. This is usually granted without cost as it also benefits the performer. Day-of-performance issues that should be clarified include who will provide the necessary equipment such as stage, lighting and sound. If parking and a prep area for the entertainer are needed, this should be described in detail. It is common for entertainers to sell merchandise. How this will be handled, along with the type of merchandise that will be sold, should also be listed.

A contract is like a seat belt in a vehicle. It probably won't be needed. However, if it *is* needed and not there, the consequences can be severe. This is true even when working with previously booked entertainers or personal friends. If there is a contract dispute, it can cause the end of a long-standing professional or personal relationship.

Discussion questions

1. Why should professional security staff be hired for events?
2. How should event organizers address environmental and social concerns of visitors?
3. What needs to be done to ensure the health of visitors?
4. How do the skills needed for managing an event differ from those needed for planning an event?
5. How should all the details involved in managing events be tracked?
6. Why are prioritizing and crisis-management skills critical for the day of the event?
7. Where could qualified employment candidates be found if staff are needed?
8. Why should a standard process be followed for interviewing and hiring employees?
9. Why is the management of independent contractors a challenge?

Case

A contract can be your best friend

Why don't event organizers always use contracts? There are two reasons. First, they believe it will take too much money and time. The second is, they don't want to think about everything that could possibly go wrong. Here are five reasons why a contract can be your best friend.

- Remove uncertainty: By clearly setting out expectations, event organizers can spend energy managing the event and not wondering what will happen if something goes wrong.
- Outline obligations: What if there is a disagreement with the caterer or entertainer? The contract will specify how it will be addressed and what remedy will be employed.
- Provide for dispute resolution: If the disagreement persists, the contract will specify how the dispute will be settled rather than having to end up in a lawyer's office.
- Help end relationships: Either party to a contract may wish to end the relationship before the event takes place. The contract will specify when and how this can be done and what penalty must be paid.
- Address the unforeseen: The contract can't foresee every possibility. Natural disaster? Illness? The contract will explain what happens next

It's better to have a contract and not need it than need a contract and not have one (Boitnott 2019)!

Task: What contracts will be needed to manage my event?

Case

What if the weather doesn't cooperate?

Wrong weather should have been listed in your SWOT analysis as one of the external threats to your event that can't be controlled. This is especially true if your event is going to held outdoors. The strategy should be to assume that the weather won't cooperate, and plan accordingly. Below are some problems that can be faced and possible solutions.

- Rain: If an event is small, there can be a backup indoor venue that can be used. Perhaps a local church or public building is willing to act as a standby venue. Tents will need to be rented, so you don't want to use them unnecessarily. Having an agreement with a rental company to supply tents if needed should be arranged.
- Heat: In some countries it is the sun, not clouds, that is the problem. Here again, tents can be used in at least some areas to let people get into the shade. In addition, large industrial fans and water misters can be used to cool people down.
- Wind: If wind might be a problem, make sure that any temporary structures that are being used, such as stages with backdrops, are securely tied down. Have plenty of small heavy objects, such as rocks, to weigh down piles of programs, napkins and anything else lightweight.
- Storms: Even an indoor event can be affected by loss of electricity due to storms. No electricity means no light or sound. If storms are predicted, invest in the rental of a portable generator so the show can go on (Walker 2020).

Task: What is your contingency plan if the event is disrupted by bad weather?

Event plan: Use the information from this chapter to complete the first section of the event plan outline at the end of the book.

References

Bishop, Clive. 2020. "How to Manage Risks in Tourism?" *CBI Ministry of Tourism Affairs*. June 8, 2020. https://www.cbi.eu/market-information/tourism/how-manage-risks-tourism. Accessed December 9, 2020.

Boitnott, John. 2019. "5 Says a Contract is an Entrepreneur's Best Friend." *Entrepreneur*. January 22, 2019. https://www.entrepreneur.com/article/326645. Accessed July 13, 2019.

Collins, Ty. 2020. "The Difference between Event Management and Event Planning." *VICTOR*. January 8, 2020. https://www.viktorwithak.com/event-management-vs-event-planning-explained/. Accessed October 23, 2020.

Hodges, Sam. 2017. "4 Ways to Make Your Mission and Values Statements Actually Matter". *Inc*. November 11, 2017. https://www.inc.com/sam-hodges/4-ways-to-make-your-mission-values-statements-actually-matter.html. Accessed January 22, 2021.

Lozano, Ally. 2018. "How Contracts Can Protect You and Your Business." *Forbes*. August 7, 2018. https://www.forbes.com/sites/yec/2018/08/07/how-contracts-can-protect-you-and-your-business/#3af0fcdb5f1f. Accessed February 29, 2021.

Ngata, Tina. 2019. "Cultural Appropriation of Maori Traditions is an Exercise in Entitlement and Privilege." *The Guardian*. December 4, 2019. https://www.theguardian.com/commentisfree/2019/dec/04/cultural-appropriation-of-maori-traditions-is-an-exercise-in-entitlement-and-privilege. Accessed November 5, 2020.

Rubinstein, Peter. 2020. "How the Wellness Industry is Taking Over Travel." *BBC*. February 4, 2020. https://www.bbc.com/worklife/article/20200203-how-the-wellness-industry. Accessed September 19, 2020.

Rue, Noah. 2018. "Four Ways to Manage Creative Employees." *Innovation Management*. September 5, 2018. https://innovationmanagement.se/2018/09/05/four-ways-to-manage-creative-employees/. Accessed February 23, 2020.

Stone, George S. 2019. "For Travelers Sustainability is the Word – But There Are Many Definitions for It." *National Geographic*. September 27, 2019. https://www.nationalgeographic.com/travel/features/what-sustainable-tourism-means/#close. Accessed September 21, 2020.

Walker, Mark. 2020. "Rain Plan for Outdoor Events." July 26, 2020. *EventBrite Blog UK*. https://www.eventbrite.co.uk/blog/outdoor-event-organisers-ds00/. Accessed October 19, 2020.

Chapter 9

Branding and event promotion

Abstract

Marketing is the exchange of a good or service for something of value that benefits both the seller and the buyer. Marketing involves the process of pricing, promoting and distributing a product. Both pricing and promoting events are challenging as the event is an intangible service. Event and tourism marketing now are mostly done online. When marketing events, the benefits, along with the features, are promoted. The public is interested in the values of the organization so they should be promoted. People expect organizations to also benefit the community. Branding helps the visitor to make decisions as it is a promise of the benefits they will receive. Developing the brand is a creative process that uses both words and visuals. The goal is to develop brand loyalty and gain repeat visitors. Social media allows the visitor to be part of the branding process. With social media, branding can occur before, during and after an event. Creating an event app will help the visitor navigate the event but also is a branding tool.

Marketing and events

While the study of marketing is new, marketing has always existed. After all, any time someone had a surplus of goods, they would then want to barter or sell them for something they did not have but needed. To do so, they first needed to find someone willing to make the exchange. The practice of marketing simply takes this basic human behavior and need for information and plans its strategic implementation. The marketing of events is the process of informing the potential visitor of the details of what they will experience, along with when and where the event is taking place. It will also inform the potential visitor of the benefits of attendance. Marketing an event requires more than just sending out a promotional message. Marketing an event is a process that starts with deciding what type of event will be held and who will be targeted with the promotional message. Marketing can be described as creating, communicating and delivering any product or service that provides value for both the seller and the buyer.

Marketing concepts applied to tourism events

The standard strategic model for marketing a product places an equal focus on the "four Ps" of product, place (distribution), price and promotion. Some descriptions of marketing also include the "Ps" of people and presentation. However, when applied to the marketing of events, this model must be adjusted. The event as a product can only be experienced or consumed by attending where it is located. Consequently the product is also the place. The venue is not an afterthought but a critical component of the experience of attendance.

Price is more challenging for marketing an event. It is common for events to have different price levels. For example, an expensive event, such as an opera festival, can be produced while at the same time less expensive events, such as concerts in the park for people who can't or don't wish to buy a ticket for the expensive performance, can be provided. As a result, when marketing events, price is not the primary strategic focus.

The promotion component of marketing strategy is essential when producing events (Lee Yohn 2019). Developing a promotional strategy for an event is challenging because much of what the event has to offer visitors is an intangible experience rather than a tangible product that can be examined before purchase through sight and touch. The intangible benefits of an experience can only be promoted indirectly through communication of an image. Even if the core event is considering worth attending, visitors will not arrive unless all the benefits of attendance are promoted. This would include ease of arrival, appropriately priced lodging, and additional activities. It should be remembered that people are not interested in a passive viewing experience. This they can have at home watching something on a screen. As people must spend considerable time and money to attend the event, unless the promotion effectively communicates everything that the visit can offer, the potential visitor may decide not to attend. Therefore, when developing a marketing plan to attract visitors to events, the emphasis must be equally on developing an event worth attending and then promoting the image of what else the visit has to offer.

Unfortunately, marketing is sometimes misunderstood as only selling, with the event organizers convincing someone to visit by falsely promising benefits that don't exist. While selling is an important part of promotion, there would be no long-term gain for tourism and lodging organizations to only focus on convincing people to visit without first ensuring it will provide the desired experience. Even if high-pressure sales techniques with false promises were used to convince visitors to attend an event, this would be a shortsighted strategy as success relies on attracting both new and repeat visitors. A visitor swayed by a sales pitch that provides an unrealistic picture of what an event has to offer would most likely be unhappy with the experience and not visit again. In addition, they would quickly go online, even while on the visit, to express their unhappiness. Potential visitors will believe another visitor before they believe the false marketing message.

Marketing and social responsibility

A modern perspective on marketing states that the exchange of a product for money should do more than just meet the needs of the buyer and seller. Marketing should also improve society as a whole by providing a wider benefit. For event marketing this would include providing value to the community in which the event is being held. Developing events that attract visitors should only be undertaken if the economic benefits improve the quality of life for residents of the destination. The economic benefits that events can provide include increasing tax revenue, attracting visitors who may someday relocate to the city and providing for economic development through encouraging new businesses that meet the needs of visitors.

The economic benefits that result from having an event will not be shared unless there is an emphasis on community and local business involvement (Duffy, Stone, Chancellor and Kline 2016). By involving the community, events can provide a product that meets the needs of visitors while improving the quality of life for the residents. In addition, by involving local businesses, economic benefits can be directly shared with community members. This can help overcome any objections to the event due to increased traffic or noise. Events can also provide community members with an opportunity to start businesses serving the needs of visitors.

Social media and marketing events

Before the development of social media, potential visitors had to rely on physical marketing materials or broadcast messages to learn about a destination. Potential visitors knew that tourism organizations producing the brochures or ads had a vested interest in portraying an event in a way that attracts visitors. Unfortunately, unless the potential visitor happened to know someone personally who had attended a previous event, there were few means of finding unbiased information.

Social media has changed how potential visitors decide upon their preferred event and plan their trip. Social media now gives the potential visitor the opportunity to directly access accurate and unbiased information on what an event has to offer. They can access information from review sites that are focused on specific events or more general travel review sites. They may also view videos taken by past visitors to the event or destination. Finally, they can visit social networking sites dedicated to specific destinations or events where travelers share experiences. These sites allow them to even post questions and have them answered by someone who has already been to the event or destination. All of this information can either encourage or discourage attendance.

It is true that the information on social media may not always be unbiased. Some postings may be negative because someone had a bad experience for reasons that had nothing to do with the event, such as personal relationship problems. Nevertheless, because of the volume of postings, the potential visitor is able to get an overall, unbiased view of what the event has to offer. Social media allows people to share experiences and their activities even while at the event by means of digital posting, photos and videos, all of which can be easily done on their smartphone. Sharing these positive experiences extends the marketing reach of the organization.

Communicating event features, benefits and values

The marketing message will be used to communicate information on what the event offers in an effort to motivate potential visitors to attend. The three types of product knowledge that can be communicated are event features, the benefits that will be received and the values of the organization All three must be communicated in a marketing message. This message will be designed to assist potential visitors in moving through the decision-making process. The marketing message, therefore, must be created to contain information on all three.

In addition, the promotional message should communicate both rationally and emotionally. The message about features will be rational and will communicate factual information to create awareness of the event. It will communicate the details of the what, where and when of the event. The marketing message on benefits will be communicated emotionally and explain the why of attendance. This part of the message will be created to build preference over competing events by communicating the benefits that will be received by attendance. An emotional marketing message will also be used to appeal to the potential visitor's own values and sense of identity. This part of the message explains who, besides the visitor, will benefit by attendance. By communicating the features, benefits and values, the marketing message will both rationally and emotionally motivate the potential visitor to move from awareness of the event to actual attendance.

The organization presenting the event must provide in their promotional communications the appropriate type of information needed by potential visitors to help them make their attendance decision. These three levels of product knowledge can be thought of as a sequence. First, the promotional message on features answers the question of what it is. The message of benefits then communicates what it does. Finally, the message on values answers who the event will benefit besides the visitor.

The first type of information concerns the features of the product. Using an event with music performances as an example, this marketing communications would include such information as the names of performers, time and date of event, the type of music presented, physical attributes of the venue and any additional services, such as food and beverage, that will be provided. Most organizations are already skilled at providing this type information.

The second type of information concerns the bundle of emotional benefits that will be provided to consumers when they attend the event. They include such benefits as self-improvement by attaining additional knowledge about the performers and music. They also might include the benefit of a social occasion that provides relaxation and entertainment. Organizations are less skilled at providing consumers with this type of information because they believe that it is self-evident how visitors will benefit emotionally. Another reason for not communicating this information in marketing is that the organization does not understand why people attend; they just hope they will do so. In this case, more research needs to be conducted to understand the motivations of visitors.

The third type of information needed by consumers concerns what values are associated with attending the event (Lobaugh 2019). Visitors may be motivated to attend a live music concert because it satisfies a personal value such as supporting local musicians. It is known that people who attend want organizations to support the community. When planning the event, emphasizing a social concern will help build attendance. This can be on a small scale, with part of the proceeds being donated to schools to support music programs. Or it can be on a global scale, where it is explained how the event was planned to minimize its carbon footprint. Attendance might be a way for the individual to be involved with and support a community organization.

Promoting event features

The first step in this communication process is to develop a marketing message that provides information about the features of the event. For example, potential visitors must know where the event is located. They will also need communication on the different costs involved in attending the event along with the availability of food. Factual information also needs to be provided on how to attend the event, including transportation options. The availability of lodging, along with links for easy booking, should be communicated. Other features that a rational promotion message might include would be information on the type and location of the venue, the entertainment agenda, planned activities and other nearby attractions such as sports, shopping, gardens, amusement parks and museums that might be visited. Also included will be information on how to obtain additional information on attractions not in the immediate vicinity.

This type of information is factual and therefore easy to communicate. The promotional message on features is particularly important when an event is being held in a location that has not been known for hosting events.

Event marketers will use this message to first build awareness of the event. To effectively create awareness, the rational promotional message must be consistent, as it may take repeated hearings before it is noticed and remembered. This consistent message should communicate a simplified version of the features the event has to offer. A promotional message that communicates too much information on everything the event offers will only confuse the potential visitor. After catching the attention of the potential visitor, additional information can be provided.

Possible features that might be included in additional promotion information would include the scenic location where the event is being held. It might also include the availability of nearby specialty shops and unique dining experiences. Local culture and artists that are part of the community where the event is being held can also be promoted. However, first the core features of the event must be promoted. The additional features simply add more reasons to attend.

Promoting event benefits

Besides information on the features of the event, potential visitors also need to know about the benefits a visit offers. Therefore, the marketing message also needs to communicate whether the event offers excitement, relaxation, adventure, education, recreation or culture. This will be an emotional message that will communicate the benefits offered using photos, images and online testimonials from past visitors. The marketing message might promote that family fun will be experienced at an event showcasing experiences with live animals, such as fun at a children's petting zoo. The benefit of excitement might be promoted at an event that involves a highly anticipated sporting event. The benefit of status might be promoted with the opportunity of seeing a special exhibit at a museum. The opportunity to socialize with other wine fans might be promoted as the reason to attend a wine-tasting event at a local winery. Other emotional benefits are based on building self-identity, such as a healthy lifestyle that comes from hiking a difficult trail or the prestige of being one of a limited number of people able to take a cooking class from a local chef.

Promoting event values

Besides information on the features and the benefits they provide, the marketing message also needs to communicate the values that the event embodies. This is particularly true for promoting events where the reason for attendance is often an emotional desire rather than a rational need. The marketing message might communicate emotionally that the event embodies such values as friendliness, creativity or spirituality. Because values are internal characteristics, they are usually communicated using emotional images. An image of visitors interacting with friendly local residents communicates a message on an emotional level much more effectively than only using words. The image communicates the value of community that will develop from attendance. If part of the event experience is contributing to environmental awareness, the image of last year's visitors participating in improving a hiking path should be used. This will communicate the wider benefits of attendance than just having an enjoyable experience. If the event is focused on having fun playing sports, the value might be helping local disabled children play. There is no one correct answer for what values should be communicated. While one event may be family focused another may emphasize a free-spirited lifestyle.

Decision-making based on values

People make attendance decisions based on a process that starts with an awareness of the event's features. The process then moves to analyzing the benefits these features provide. Potential visitors will then consider the emotional component of what the purchase of the product will mean to them based on their values. Much more than in the past, consumers today base their decisions on whether the values of the organization and the event match their own. These organizational values then reinforce the self-identity of the visitor (Butler 2018).

Promotional message

- Features to build awareness: Experience nature, learn to cook, hear music.
- Benefits to create preference: Fun, relaxation, togetherness, learning.
- Values to reflect self-identity: Family time, spiritual renewal, build community.

Branding the event

Branding is the process of using very few words and visuals that together will communicate to potential visitors the image of the event along with the features, benefits and values it has to offer. While the words and visuals used together are simply thought of as a brand, the term "brand name" actually refers to the words while the term "brand mark" refers to the visuals or the logo.

A brand is communicated in the hope that it will change the perceptions of a product. The visuals and words are designed to affect the feelings, beliefs and perceptions of the consumer. The branded event message should represent what the event has to offer the visitor. This brand message will then reinforce existing positive believes based on what the potential visitor has seen and heard on social media. It is also used to change negative feelings and perceptions of the event, which, again, may have been acquired through online browsing. An event promotional campaign that uses inconsistent messages will simply confuse the potential visitor as to the features and benefits that they will receive.

The brand message makes a promise to the potential visitor of what they will experience when they visit. The value of the event brand is reinforced every time the promise is kept. An effective brand image cannot be created by the organization unless it honestly describes the features, benefits and values of the event. The value of the brand is then reinforced by social media posted by past visitors. The use of a branded message reduces risk to the visitor. With so many competing events and little time for product research, potential visitors are more likely to purchase a known branded event than to try an unknown event. Because branding helps to communicate the event's competitive advantage, the brand acts as a quick reminder of what the event has to offer.

The development of a brand is a creative process that can require a high level of expertise. If no one involved in the process of planning the event has this level of creativity it may be necessary to seek the advice of a marketing professional. Despite the time and effort required, creating a brand that will come to be identified with the event is a worthwhile use of resources.

The purpose of the brand is to become an expression of the values of the organization (Greyser and Urde 2019). For example, consumers may care deeply about poverty in economically underdeveloped countries but may feel that as individuals there is nothing they can do to solve the problem. However, by attending an event where the vendors are selling products that provide employment in such countries, they now can think of themselves as someone who not only cares, but also takes action to alleviate poverty. Both a marketing message on the product benefits and a brand image that speaks to the values of the consumer are necessary to sell a product in a crowded marketplace. A well-developed brand image communicates both rational facts needed to make a decision but also an emotional message to the visitor that provides a preview of what they will feel when they attend. In addition, the brand communicates the values of the organization.

Branding process

- Create image: Such as traditional, trendy, vibrant, calming, exotic, familiar.
- Write words: Use fewer than ten words to describe the event and its benefit.
- Placement: Use brand on all printed and social media.

Branding helps with the decision process

There is another purpose to branding. People can find online an almost unlimited variety of events that they can attend. While this may be seen as an advantage, it makes the decision of what to attend difficult. Not all potential visitors have the time or interest to do the research to find an event that will provide both the desired benefits and match their values. Branding helps solve this dilemma. Because people lack trust in traditional marketing messages, they prefer to place their trust in brands. The most trusted resource for information on brands is still personal recommendations of family and friends. When these are unavailable, people use social media, including bloggers and influencers, to learn about brands.

Because the event product is intangible, the brand image communicates the type of experience that the event will provide. It is part of the guarantee that the event will be as it is represented in the promotion. There is an old saying that you can't know a book by its cover. In branding of intangible experiences, this idea is turned on its head. It is the cover, or brand image, that must quickly and accurately inform the potential customer of the contents. In fact, even the design of the venue can be used to express the brand image. The exterior signage and interior design should also reflect the ambience of the brand whether edgy, trendsetting, family friendly or traditional. Even small details, such as the ticket design, should incorporate the brand image.

A means to start creating a branding message is to think of the adjectives that describe the event experience. The event might be thought of as trendy, safe, fashionable, exciting, calming, healthy or any combination of these or other words. Brands have emotional connotations with consumers, so the words should also be emotional. To get design ideas for the visuals that will be used, there are many websites that show brand logos. Of course, these should not be copied, but they can be used to spark inspiration.

If consumers have developed brand preference, it is said that brand equity has been created. Because people associate positive attributes to the brand, it has value that is stolen if another organization uses the same brand name or image. Worse, another organization may devalue the brand by providing inferior events with the same brand name. Therefore an organization must protect its brand through having the rights to the words and any logo registered, if this is possible in their country.

Brand loyalty

The motivation for branding an event is not just to get a visitor to attend once. It is instead to have them develop a relationship with the event so that they attend again. This relationship is known as brand loyalty. If visitors are brand loyal, they will make an event their first choice when they decide what to attend. They are also more likely to try any new type of events that the organization develops as they trust the brand. Lastly, they will recommend to their friends that they support the organization and community by attending the event. Such brand loyal consumers will be more likely to post positive reviews online.

Branding builds loyalty by communicating the image of the event's mission and not just the benefits of attendance. Rather than just a promotional message, the brand embodies the mission of what the event hopes to achieve. If visitors believe in the mission, they are more likely to repeatedly attend the event as they are secure in the knowledge that they will receive the benefits that are promoted.

Developing brand loyalty takes time and effort, which is worth it because consumers prefer to purchase based on brands as it makes the attendance decision less risky. Of course brands can be used to make people aware of the product's features and benefits. Brands can also be used to make people aware of the organization's values. Often consumers wish to purchase products from organizations whose values align with their own. Brands make this easier to do.

The first product purchase may be based only on the fact that consumers are aware of a brand so they want to try the product. Building this awareness into brand loyalty is worthwhile as a consumer will then purchase the product, rather than purchase a similar product of which they have never heard, even if the similar product has a lower price. Sales incentives, which are short-term reductions in price or product gifts, can then be used to motivate repeat purchases until the consumer develops brand loyalty.

Social media and branding

The branding of the event should quickly communicate the event name and when and where it will be held. Most importantly, it will communicate how the event is unique and differentiated from other similarly themed events. This is challenging to accomplish in a few words and perhaps a single image. When creating the brand image, a critical consideration is how it will be used on social media sites (Kundariya 2019).

The branded message and visuals should remain as similar as possible across all social media platforms. The layout may need to be changed to conform to the restraints inherent in the way different social media platforms present information. The components that will likely remain the same include the logo and slogan while the amount of words used will vary. Using an image-sharing social media site, such as Instagram, means that there may be little wording used while a Facebook posting can include more. What can remain the same across platforms is the colors, fonts and style of language.

Color and font choice both communicate meaning and should not be based simply on what appeals to the organization. For example, bright colors will communicate excitement while soft colors will bring feelings of relaxation. Over time a brand can become associated with a color. Fonts also convey meaning. There are fonts that are considered trendy and even edgy while other fonts are more traditional. The term "persona" is often used in social media branding. The dictionary describes the term as an assumed role. This is misleading because the persona must honestly represent the organization, as the public is quick to discern a fake representation. The persona is represented by the type of language used. This might be friendly for a family-focused event. In contrast, the language used might be authoritative for an educational event. Other examples would be warm, welcoming, playful or serious. Just like individuals with strong personalities, the voice used for the social media postings should not change.

Visitor involvement in promotion

One radical difference between traditional promotion and using social media is that social media allows for the consumer to become part of the promotion process. The traditional term often used to describe this process is word-of-mouth marketing, but now this includes sharing information about events online. When using social media, it is hoped that the marketing message that is communicated by the organization gets recommunicated online by visitors. In the process, the visitor becomes a brand advocate. While personal discussions about products have always taken place between individuals, online communication amplifies this process.

Not only is it amplified, the message will also be changed by consumers who are communicating about the brand and product. In fact, some individuals will become so knowledgeable about categories of products that they will have followers that use them as sources of product information. These influencers may have blogs, video channels, their own social media sites, or all of them. Organizations that wish to have their events mentioned must build into their marketing strategies a means of providing event information to these influencers so they can become advocates. Creating brand advocates is not something that just happens. Instead it must be an active part of a promotion strategy. To create brand advocates, the organization must first establish the trust that they both produce an excellent event and then establish a personal relationship with influencers.

Event branding before, during and after

Promoting the event on social media before the event will help to build excitement for those who are already planning to attend. It will also create interest for those who have not yet made the attendance decision. This promotion may start with an early announcement of the date of the event. This posting should appear at the same time on all the organization's social media sites.

These postings should also include any hashtags that are created to allow people to closely follow additional announcements. The hashtags can be part of future postings to announce speakers, entertainment or activities. Rather than send all the information at one time, the organization can build interest by spacing out the postings so that each will receive sufficient notice. It can even be "teased" by sending a post that information about a surprise entertainment offering will be revealed at a specific date. The same can be done with activities. When announced, these postings can include links that will show the entertainment and activity so that the potential visitor can sample what they will experience. Lastly, social media can be used to announce limited-offer deals on pricing. Tweeting that a lower price with an end date where it will no longer be offered can be very effective in motivating early ticket purchase.

Social media promotion designed to reinforce branding is not finished when the event starts. It continues during the event to connect the audience with each other and to share with people who could not attend. This is to ensure visitors return and to motivate those not present to attend the next event. This can be done by posting photos of visitors enjoying what the event offers. Using video clips that also contain quotes on what the event means to people can be shared immediately and also used in future content marketing.

After the event, the branding continues. First, it can be used to send a thank-you to everyone who attended. After all, it was their presence that made the event a success. Everyone can also be sent a posting with the best photos and testimonials about the event. This will reinforce the attendance decision and remind those who did not attend of the fun they missed. This can then be combined with an offer for discounted tickets for the next event if purchased immediately. Finally, a short survey can be sent simply asking what people liked best and for ideas for improving the next event.

How social media can be used to brand

- Before event: Date countdown, hashtags, tease activity announcements.
- During event: Post visitor photos, videos or activities.
- After event: Testimonials, post thank-you notes.

Creating an event app

It is now possible for organizations to develop an app for their event without hiring a specialized company to do so. Someone in the organization familiar with technology can use a software template to create an app specific to an event. One of the main reasons for doing so is to stay in communication with the attendee before, during and even after the event. First the app can be used for sending out promotional messages about new entertainment or activities that have been added. A countdown feature can remind potential attendees how much time they have to register and then how much time there is until the start of the event. Visitors can use the app to purchase tickets and register for the activities. Users of the app can be sent messages with helpful information such as expected weather and any transportation issues.

Any promotional information that appears on the organization's social media sites can also be posted onto the app. Contests for extra perks while at the event can be added to build excitement. One of the most useful features of an app is the ability to communicate and to network. The app can allow visitors to ask questions about the event. Apps can also be designed to allow visitors to communicate with each other before, during and after the event. Since one of the reasons for attending an event is to socialize, this can be a very useful feature.

Discussion questions

1. Why is pricing a service such as an event challenging?
2. How does the fact that an event is a service affect promotion?
3. Why should organizations emphasize their values in marketing messages?
4. How does the use of social media change the marketing of events?
5. What is the difference between the features, benefits and values of any event?
6. How does branding help the visitor?
7. What role do the values of the organization play in visitor decision-making?
8. How are visitors involved in branding on social media?
9. How can events be branded before, during and after?

Case

What event elements can be branded?

Customers who emotionally connect with a brand are three times more likely to purchase again and to recommend the product to other consumers. This is why attention must be paid to not only developing a brand image but also communicating it to visitors in every way possible. This communication must be consistent with the same style of words, visuals, fonts and colors. Of course, your brand will be on your printed material and social media sites. Here are some other ideas.

- Décor: Make the logo part of your décor. It can be enlarged onto a wall where your visitors can pose for photos.
- Drink: Create a signature cocktail or nonalcoholic drink and then name it after yourself.
- Food: Create a snack that fits the theme of the event and then provide a printed card with your logo and the recipe.
- Big Things: If the budget will allow, or sponsors can be found, provide branded umbrellas if it rains or warm wraps if it is cold. If it is hot, branded paper fans can be provided.
- Small Things: Brand your pens, napkins, drink stir sticks, cups and tickets. If the brand can fit on it, brand it!

Just make sure that the brand is consistent across all uses. Of course, it may have been simplified to fit onto small objects, but it should still be recognized as your brand (Higgins 2019).

Task: The ten ways your brand can be used before, during and after the event.

Case

From planning to visiting consists of micro-moments

According to research conducted by Google the travel decision-making process consists of three distinct stages. During the first step people are less likely to immediately research a brand name but will first start looking for a solution to their need. For travel this means a generalized search on where to go or what to do. Only then will potential visitors start looking at a specific branded event. Google has identified the following three steps that they call micro-moments when making the travel decision.

- I want to get away: This stage starts with using a search engine. To engage the interest of potential visitors, short, easy-to-digest information must appear in search engine results on the type of event or destination. It is visuals and videos that are now clicked on, not the written word.
- Time to make a plan: Once the potential visitor has found information on an event of interest in a generalized search, they will find research on the specific event. Once on the event social media or website, they want specific information on the what, where and when of the event.
- Let's book it: When it comes to booking tickets, a majority of people searching on a mobile device will then switch to a computer to finish the booking. This is where the visitor can be lost to a competitor. To not disrupt the process, the organization must make it easier to book on a mobile device (Sherwood 2018).

Task: What kind of branded information should be seen on search engine resutls so that potential visitors will then go on to my event site for more information?

Event plan: Use the information from this chapter to complete the first section of the event plan outline at the end of the book.

References

Butler, Adam. 2018. "Do Customers Really Care about Your Environmental Impact?" *Forbes*. November 21, 2018. https://www.forbes.com/sites/forbesnycouncil/2018/11/21/do-customers-really-care-about-your-environmental-impact/#3a646ba4240d. Accessed December 11, 2020.

Duffy, L.N., G. Stone, H. Charles Chancellor, and C.S. Kline. 2016. "Tourism Development in the Dominican Republic: An Examination of the Economic Impact to Coastal Households." *Tourism and Hospitality Research* 16(1), 35–49.

Greyser, Stephen, and Mats Urde. 2019. "What Does Your Corporate Brand Stand For?" *Harvard Business Review*. January 2019. https://hbr.org/2019/01/what-does-your-corporate-brand-stand-for. Accessed December 21, 2020.

Higgins, Ronnie. 2019. "The Ultimate Guide to Event Branding." *EventBright Blog.* March 21, 2019. https://www.eventbrite.com/blog/ultimate-guide-to-event-branding-ds00/. Accessed October 10, 2019.

Kundariya, Harikrishna. 2019. "A Step by Step Guide to Build a Brand Using Social Media." *Entrepreneur.* https://www.entrepreneur.com/article/341181. Accessed December 4, 2020.

Lee Yohn, Denise. 2019. "Why Marketing Matters Now More than Ever." January 8, 2019. *Forbes.* https://www.forbes.com/sites/deniselyohn/2019/01/08/marketing-matters-now-more-than-ever/?sh=645b5150117a. Accessed November 19, 2020.

Lobaugh, Kasey. 2019. "A Deeper Dive into Modern Consumer Behavior." *Wall Street Journal.* October 23, 2019. https://deloitte.wsj.com/cmo/2019/10/23/a-deeper-dive-into-modern-consumer-behavior/. Accessed September 13, 2020.

Sherwood, Pete. 2018. "How Travel Companies Can Nail Market Segmentation." *Gravitate.* September 13, 2018. https://www.gravitatedesign.com/blog/tourism-market-segmentation-101/. Accessed August 3, 2020.

Chapter 10

Promoting with traditional media

Abstract

Traditional forms of promotional communication include advertising, public relations, sales incentives and personal selling. All of these are still used but are now combined with social media. Marketing promotion has now been redefined into paid, owned, earned and shared. Paid media includes promotional messages placed on social media purchased by the organization. Owned media is the organization's own social media sites. Earned media includes consumers promoting the event on their social media. Shared media results when consumers share the promotional message across platforms. The AIDA model explains how promotion is used to attract attention, develop interest, create desire and motivate action. Social media has changed the communication model as it allows direct contact back from the receiver to the sender of the message. Advertising is now placed digitally on social media and websites. Public relation messages are now posted online. Sales incentives are used to motivate immediate purchase. Personal selling involves solving a problem for the visitor.

New media model

Prior to the development of social media, marketing promotion was described as having five distinct methods to communicate a marketing message, each used for a specific purpose. These methods are still used today but in combination with social media. In the past, most organizations and businesses relied on advertising to promote a product. Public relations, sales incentives and personal selling were also methods of sharing a marketing message.

Advertising, either print or broadcast, is defined as paid, one-way mass communication in which the company or organization is identified as the sponsor of the message.

121

In addition to advertising, public relations is used to have a print or broadcast message communicated by another media outlet not controlled by the organization. Public relations differs in that it uses indirect methods of communication to increase awareness of the product or to change negative attitudes about the product. It was thought that people would believe another media source more than the company producing a marketing message.

Sales incentives are short-time promotion offers that are used to motivate purchase. They include methods of motivation including contests, two-for-one offers, and free gifts with purchase. Sales incentives used to motivate consumers to purchase a product also include pricing discounts that are temporary and often targeted at first-time purchasers. Personal selling is communicating the marketing message to one person at a time. Complicated and expensive products often use paid staff using personal selling to communicate the marketing message. For other products, all staff are expected to communicate benefits of products when in contact with the public. Each of these four tools has a specific role to play in motivating consumers to purchase.

At first, this list may seem out of date because of the prevalence of using social media for communicating marketing messages. It should be remembered that social media is simply a means of communication, not the message itself. The traditional forms of promotion are still important to understand and use. The advantage of traditional media is that it can engage people's attention when they are not focused on a screen (Tama 2019). The amount of traditional media versus social media to use when trying to engage attention and motivate purchase depends on the targeted visitor segment. Only relying on social media is setting aside many other useful means of motivation.

Combining promotional messages

Social media is now used in combination with traditional forms of promotional communication, whether print, broadcast or in person. Tourism organizations will use more than one promotional method to communicate the event promotional message. In fact, it is better if multiple methods of communication are used as it is difficult to get the attention of the consumer. What is important for marketers to remember is that no matter what combination of promotional methods is used, the same message needs to be communicated.

The example of an Italian food festival can be used to describe how these methods could be used in combination. Posters would be distributed advertising the marketing message of "No need to visit Italy for great pasta!" along with an image of families happily eating. A radio broadcast could be prepared with an announcer describing the event with Italian music in the background. Public relations press releases with festival information could be sent to local newspapers. Sales incentives would include a discounted weekend package with a free bottle of Italian wine. All staff at hotels and visitor bureaus would be trained to sell the festival. What is different now is that the posters would also show up on Instagram, the radio broadcast would involve a podcast, press releases would be sent to influencers, sales incentives would be promoted on Facebook and the staff would be trained using a YouTube video.

Redefining marketing promotion

The development of social media was first used as a means of personal communication between friends. It was soon noticed by organizations that one of the topics discussed by friends was their preference for products. Organizations, some sooner than others, understood that they needed to influence these online discussions. They started to do so by creating their own social media sites. These sites became more effective in communicating the marketing message than many of the traditional forms of communication. As a result, the types of marketing communication were rethought. They are now defined as paid, owned, earned and shared media

Types of media

- Paid media: Paid promotional messages placed on social media by the company.
- Owned media: Company's own social media sites.
- Earned media: Consumers promoting the company's product on their social media.
- Shared media: Consumers sharing information across platforms.

Paid media

Paid social media includes the use of online display ads, search ads and social media ads. Display ads are marketing messages that are meant to be seen online. For a tourism event this would include banner ads that appear on websites associated with either the destination or type of event. The consumer is looking for the content on the website but is hopefully attracted by the banner ad to seek more information about the event. Search ads appear on search page results as sponsored links. When a consumer is searching for information on events, the search algorithm will present a list of useful links. The organization can pay to have their link appear at the top of the page. Social media ads can be displayed around specific types of sites just like display ads. They differ in that they can also appear in social media feeds. With paid social media the company pays for the ad placement but can control all the visuals and wording.

Using paid media sends a marketing message to the general public. Paid media does not guarantee that the target market segment will decide to attend the event. Instead, as a result of hearing the message, it is hoped that some potential visitors will seek out more event information by visiting owned media controlled by the organization.

Owned media

Owned media is the use of social media technology to send a marketing message to both promote and build a community around the product and organization. Websites, social networking sites, photo- or video-sharing sites and other social media platforms created and controlled by the organization are examples of owned media. In addition, blogging and podcasts would be considered other examples. Owned media differs from paid media in that the promotional message is on social media sites created by the organization aimed at a specific target market segment.

These owned social media sites are also designed to encourage a response. Owned media, while still communicating the organization's marketing message, also asks for the public to respond with their own opinions and ideas about the event. As a result, conversations are started where the potential visitor may agree or disagree with the promotional message. Because the organization will then need to respond to these comments, owned media takes more time and energy than paid media. However, it is much more effective in engaging interest, building trust and developing a community around the event than paid media.

Earned media

Earned media is outside of the control of the organization. It includes comments posted about the product on other social networking sites, bloggers who write about the product and customer reviews. An example of earned media is a video clip of people visiting a past event that is made by a visitor and then posted on YouTube for anyone to see.

Earned media can be favorable to the company or it can be unfavorable. While the organization should monitor earned media and respond where appropriate, it in no way controls or even guides the content. Of course, the organization is pleased with positive earned media. If the earned media is not positive, the company must react, either by countering negative information or improving the product if the complaints are valid.

Shared media

The newest category of promotional media is shared. Shared media is anytime someone reacts to what the organization posts by sharing it with others. This has developed because social media users not only respond to the postings of the organization but also share information among themselves. This can be as simple as forwarding a product review or a retweet of a comment. Shared media can develop into a self-organized fan community.

These fan communities will have their own websites and social media platforms that have no connection with the company that produces the product. Using these sites, the members of the community will share examples of how the product can be used and will even answer questions from potential purchasers about the product. These fan communities promote the product without any input from the company.

Product review sites are another example of shared media. Because these sites are not controlled by the organization, they are trusted by the public. When individuals complain on the organization's owned social networking site, it is easy for a response to be posted. However, they may also complain to other potential visitors on an independent product review site. There is a difference in how product review readers react to negative reviews that should be understood. When negative reviews of practical products meant for everyday use are read, they are likely to be believed. However, negative reviews of products that are purchased because of the pleasure they give, such as attending tourism events, are more likely to be dismissed by readers as resulting from the internal bias of the reviewer, not a problem with the product. Readers of this type of negative review are more likely to understand that beauty is in the eye of the beholder (Sen and Lerman 2007).

Influencer marketing comes under the category of shared media. Influencers are people who post content on social media sites that are followed by others. The content may be about any category including shopping, sports, fashion, art or events. These influencers use blog posts, share visual images, and post videos to share their opinions and product recommendations. Influencers that have thousands of followers are sometimes approached by companies to try out products that they sell. The company can't control whether the influencer will share positive or negative information. Tourism organizations can use local influencers with smaller followings and ask them to share information (Dermoudy 2018). These influencers, even more than those with national followings, are believed to give honest feedback about the product because they need to maintain their credibility with their followers.

Use of media to motivate purchase

The purpose of paid media is to build awareness and attract potential visitors to owned media. The purpose of owned media is to get people to create earned media by communicating with each other about the product. Earned media is the mention of the company and the product on other social media sites. The next step is to have shared media. In order to generate shared media, the organization will use content marketing. This is the placement of information on owned media that will either educate or entertain the consumer. This can be informational content created by the organization or news from elsewhere that is shared.

Action, interest, desire, action – AIDA

A promotional campaign is developed with the objective of encouraging the consumer to take some form of action. This action might be to attend an event or purchase a product. However, motivating a potential visitor to take the action of attending an event is rarely a one-step process. Because people are surrounded by promotional messages from both traditional and social media, they tend to tune them out. To reach people in this environment it is necessary to understand how a person goes from awareness of an event to making the visit decision.

The AIDA model explains this process of attracting attention, developing interest, creating desire and motivating action. Because of the many promotional messages that people experience every day, they tend to go unnoticed. As a result, simply getting the attention of a potential visitor with any promotional message is a challenge. To do so, the message must speak directly to the visitors' needs and desires. Generalized messages that an event is being held will not be heard. Instead, a message aimed at a specific visitor segment must be used. The message should quickly attract the eye and engage the viewer long enough to communicate. This is particularly challenging because of the practice of multi-screening (Buckley 2019). For example, when watching a video on their computer, the viewer is often simultaneously looking at information on their phone. At the same time, they may also be listening to their children. Because of all these distractions, even the most compelling message about an event has only a few seconds to be noticed by the potential visitor.

However, getting attention is only the first step in the process of motivating attendance. The promotional message must now cause the person to develop an interest in learning more about the event. To do so, the style of the communication must display an affinity with the psychographic characteristics, values, attitudes and lifestyles of the targeted visitors. It must connect emotionally and not just with rationale factual information. Depending on the type of event, the promotional message might use humor, dramatic visuals or personal testimonials on the benefits of attendance to develop interest. Social media content postings incorporating these words and visuals can also be effective in gaining interest.

After the promotion has caught the attention and developed interest, the next step is to create in the potential visitor a desire for the event. At this step in the process content about the event posted both by the organization and the public becomes critical. There are two ways this can be accomplished. The first is through reinforcing messages from other visitors. This might be postings from past visitors or visitors who have just booked and are looking forward to their visit. The promotional message plus this type of content must convince the visitor that no competing event can meet their needs. The second way is for the organization to provide an incentive to make an immediate purchase. Incentives such as providing a discount or premium if purchase is made quickly can be used. This could be a limited time offer of a percentage off or providing an extra benefit such as a free beverage or transportation.

It might be assumed that after creating desire, the potential visitor would purchase a ticket to attend automatically. However, this is not the case. The organization must make the action step as easy as possible by providing all needed information on how to purchase a ticket including a physical or online address. All necessary information on location, transportation and a contact for additional help needs to be available. If the potential customer should have any difficulty in making all the necessary steps to attendance, the process will come to a stop.

AIDA process

- Attention: Getting message heard through clutter.
- Interest: Communicating benefits that appeal to segment.
- Desire: Using incentives to separate out message.
- Action: Making purchase process easy.

New communication model

The standard communication model applied to the purchase process was based on a sender, a message sent via media, and a receiver. First, the sender developed a direct message using a form of media. This message was sent to a receiver who was waiting to listen. This message had to break through interference, or noise, to be heard correctly by the receiver. If there was too much noise the message could be misinterpreted or not heard at all. The only way that the sender knew if the message was received and understood was through feedback from the receiver to the sender. Of course, this feedback was indirect, the purchase of the product. Outside of having a telephone number to call, there were few other ways for the organization to hear directly from the receiver of the promotional message.

The use of social media has changed the process. It still starts with the sender developing and communicating the message. However, with online communication, the message is available not just to the intended receiver but to anyone else who should notice it. Social media now allows the receiver to easily communicate back to the sender of the message as to whether the message was understood and accepted. If receivers find the message of interest, they can now resend the message to others. Because the message can easily be reposted, there is less concern with interference as the receivers can consume the message at their convenience.

While social media makes communication easier to send, it makes it more difficult to be heard because there is a staggering number of messages online. Therefore, any message sent about an event needs to entertain or assist a potential visitor in some way. Members of the public are most likely to ignore any promotional message that simply communicates that they should attend. With an abundance of events from which to choose, each of which is saying "visit me," it is understandable that these messages will simply not be heard. Therefore, the promotional message needs to contain information of use to the receiver in the hope that once this information is consumed, the receivers will, on their own, seek out more information on the event. The consumer must hear the marketing message from between five and seven times before it is remembered (Peek 2020). This cannot be the same message communicated through the same channel, which will then be ignored, but rather new messages communicated through different channels.

If the promotional message is of interest to the receiver, they will resend it to others. This will not be merely a passive resending, but will also contain the original receiver's comments they have added. These secondary receivers may then again amplify the message. Receivers may also amplify the promotional message by posting it on blogs and online review sites. These indirect marketing messages are of more interest to potential visitors than the organization's direct marketing messages. Since these comments are so influential, organizations must respond to these messages whether they are positive or negative.

Advertising and public relations

Advertising has historically been defined as one-way, impersonal communication. Before social media, it is probably what most people thought of first when asked about promotion. In fact, the words promotion and advertising are still often used interchangeably. While in the past advertising was limited to the traditional forms of print and broadcast, such as newspapers, magazines, radio and TV, it also includes inexpensive methods such as flyers and posters. The marketing message can also be placed on coffee cups and the back of ticket stubs. Bus placards and posters on buildings may seem old-fashioned but are still effective. Advertising can now appear in such unlikely places as being trailed by an airplane or on the back of a public lavatory door.

The main types of traditional advertising media are broadcast and print. Broadcast advertising includes both television and radio. Broadcast advertising may not be possible for a small organization because of both the expense of production and cost of media time. However, print as a communication method should be considered. While advertising campaigns using publications with broad reach can be costly, tourism organizations should not forget that many people still check the local paper, either in print or online, for both news and advertisements. In addition, tourism publications, which are often widely distributed, are possible sites for the placement of advertisements. These types of publications have the advantage that most are specific to a geographic area or a type of event.

While magazines still exist, many are now read online. The advantage of using magazine websites is that many are targeted narrowly at very specific lifestyle or special interest groups. The visitor target market segment may be defined by psychographic characteristics such as sustainable living or an interest in a particular art form such as bluegrass music. If this is true, there is most likely a magazine targeted at this same visitor segment. If it is affordable, placing an advertisement may be a wise investment. Online advertising on social networking sites should also be considered. When designing for ads for use on social media, striking photos which immediately grab the attention must be used. People are particularly likely to click on video links.

Creativity is needed to think of how the potential visitor can be reached with the message using advertising. While ads on social media are the focus of much attention, other simple and inexpensive methods continue to be effective (Wrobelewski 2018). A poster, flyer or brochure can catch the attention of the visitor market segment if strategically placed where they will be noticed. These methods have historically been used to advertise events and performances and are still an effective method for communicating a marketing message to attract visitors. These low-cost methods can be successful if the message and visuals are targeted at a specific segment.

What all the forms have in common is that they are used to communicate words and images to build awareness of the product. This message must be concise and quickly understood as people's attention spans are very short. It is then hoped that the potential visitor will seek out additional information on websites, social media or through personal contact.

Advertising is rarely used in isolation as it is not enough to stimulate immediate sale. Instead, it is used to motivate the consumer to find out more about the product. Because advertising must be concise, the information it provides is usually limited to the product name and a marketing message that describes its competitive advantage. It tries to quickly answer what the event is and why should someone attend. The advertisement will also explain how the visitor can obtain additional information by including links to social media sites or a phone number.

Successful advertising works on both a rational and an emotional level. The rational message concerns the events features and the benefits they provide. The emotional message answers the question of why the visitor should attend. For some products, the rational message is communicated first. These products are usually ones that solve a specific and immediate problem. If it is winter and someone has no heat in their home, they want to know immediately from the information in the advertising who can fix the heater. However, tourism and event products usually do not solve an immediate need. They will most likely use advertising with an emotional marketing message to promote purchase. This message may remind the potential visitors that they are overstressed or bored and then present the event as providing a benefit that will either relax or excite.

Public relations

All organizations perform the task of public relations, even if it is not a formal part of their promotion strategy. This is because every organization wants a positive reputation in their community. Public relations is a means of formalizing this approach so that communication from the organization includes information on the positive impact the event will have on the community. In addition, public relations can be used to counter negative information. Finally, public relations is used to encourage other media to speak positively about the organization and the upcoming event. The tools that can be used include press releases, sponsorship and charitable giving. The difference between advertising and public relations is the messenger. Advertising is communicated directly from the organization to the public. Of course, the public expects that the organization will only have positive messages about the event. Public relations is other media outlets or people of influence talking about the organization and event. Hopefully, the communication will be positive but the organization cannot control the message.

One of the tools of public relations has historically been the press release, which was written and sent to print and broadcast media. Now the press release will most likely be in digital form. It may still be emailed to traditional media broadcast and print outlets in the hope that they will mention the event but it may also be sent to bloggers who write about events. In addition, the press release will be posted on the organization's own website and social media sites in hopes that it will be passed on, therefore becoming shared media. To be an effective means of communication, the press release must be written with the readers in mind so that it persuades them that the event the organization is planning is of interest. To do so it must grab the reader's attention in seconds using the headline and the first few sentences.

The organizers of the event may choose to sponsor a local charity as a beneficiary of the event. What differentiates this from advertising is that the sponsorship has a community purpose. Placing an ad about a sporting event is a form of advertising. Having other media sources communicate the fact that part of the event program is supporting a nonprofit youth sports league is public relations. It is hoped that members of the public will be impressed by the fact that the organization is living up to its mission and values and, as a result, they are more likely to attend. If not, they at least are left with a favorable impression of the organization that they might communicate online to others. Social media owners and managers of companies are now known to the public, which expects them to take a stand on social and political issues (Doerr 2018). They are now considered leaders of their communities not just of their organizations, and the public expects them to use their voice to produce social change.

Closely related to sponsorship is charitable giving. It is common policy in for-profit companies that part of their revenue be used to support a charitable cause. This information is then communicated to the public as part of public relations. If this is possible, the organization might choose a charity that is close to its mission or a charity important to the visitor market segment being targeted. Of course, it may not be possible to donate in the form of cash. Instead, the organization may donate free event tickets to a local charity. They may also provide free transportation to the event for elderly residents.

Sales incentives and personal selling

Sales promotions are used to build interest in buying a product by providing a reason for immediate purchase. While the ideas can be considered simple and are certainly not new, they continue to work because they respond to a basic human desire for a "good deal." They have always included such ideas as free gifts with purchase, contests and discounts. The existence of the incentives was communicated using traditional methods of promotion. Now the same methods of sales incentives are successfully adapted for use on social media. In fact, they are even more successful because everyone wants to share when they get a good deal (Weisberg 2019).

Sales promotions are usually limited-time offers that can be designed to target either past visitors so that they attend again or to attract new visitors. Specific sales incentives methods can also be designed to appeal to a specific target market segment. More than one incentive may be offered as what works for one group of visitors may not work for another. In addition, the cost of the incentive needs to be scaled to the cost of attending an event.

Some sales promotions offer a free gift, such as an additional product that customers receive with their purchase. For example, a small gift that is included with the purchase of an inexpensive product is appropriate. However, as the cost of the product increases, the cost of the gift that is provided must also increase. For an example, a free tote bag might be given when attending a low-cost daytime concert on a beach. A bottle of local wine might be included when an expensive ticket for an evening performance is purchased.

The cost of providing these gift incentives can be decreased by the sponsorship of local businesses that cover the cost of the gift. They then could also include information on the business. If the gift item, such as a tote bag or a drinking glass, carries the business logo, they may be willing to provide them for free. Businesses may also be willing to provide coupons for discounts that would then encourage visitors to patronize their establishments.

Finally, some sales promotions involve contests where the purchaser can win a prize. Contests have the advantage of collecting information on the potential visitors that can then be used to send future promotional messages and offers. Contests can be a very effective way to motivate purchase. Having a chance to win the opportunity to sit in preferred seats or meet a popular entertainer can motivate buying a ticket immediately rather than waiting. Some sales promotions are financial, such as a temporary reduction in price or a coupon that can be used to reduce the price of products bought at an event.

Of course, the public needs to be made aware of the available sales incentives. Information can be easily added to the organization's social media promotional campaign. In fact, sales incentive promotions can provide content that can be written about for content marketing, blog entries and tweets. Sales incentives can also use consumer-created promotion. Winners of sales incentives can be asked to post videos and photos of why they are attending, with the best winning a prize. The organization can then share these images on other social media sites.

The advantage of sales incentives is that they can be crafted to help motivate attendance during a specific time period. Incentives might be used when the event is first announced to build excitement and encourage early purchase of tickets. Another approach is to wait and use them if tickets are not selling as anticipated to increase purchases.

Personal selling

Personal selling is informing the consumer of the benefits of the event. Personal selling is not just the job of a professional salesperson; everyone in the organization is responsible for helping inform people of the event. A common misconception is that sales is convincing someone to do something they would rather not do. There would be no long-term advantage in trying to manipulate people by making false promises about the benefits of attendance. Once they attend the event, they will discover they have been misinformed. They will then go online to inform everyone else and the organization will have lost the trust of the public.

Personal selling should be done by all members of the organization, using every opportunity to inform the public with whom they come into contact about the benefits attending the event will provide. For example, ticket sellers, when they sell a ticket to the event, should recommend additional activities that might be of interest. Even the staff at an event can inform visitors of the products on offer in the gift shop or refreshment stands. To be able to sell, the people in the organization must understand all aspects of the event and be able to communicate these to anyone with whom they may come into contact.

Personal selling is communicating to any potential visitor that requests information. However, personal selling also involves being proactive and seeking opportunities to provide information. One way to do so is to communicate to other organizations. If the event is regional, this would include other tourism-related businesses in the area as they may have visitors that are looking for activities. It can also be speaking at civic organizations to spread the word about the upcoming event.

Selling to tour groups may be worth the effort, depending on the visitor segment being targeted. Some visitor segments are more interested in traveling with likeminded others. This may be older visitors who believe traveling on a tour saves them the effort of researching transportation and lodging options. They may also feel that they are safer in a group. People unfamiliar with the language and culture of an area may also be more likely to travel with a tour group.

When selling to a tour group, additional benefits should be provided. Ease of access to the venue might include a dedicated entrance gate or door for groups. Small gifts, souvenir programs and other extras might be included as an inducement. It is the tour leader who is the purchaser of tickets for their group, so they should be the focus of personal selling. The tour leader or company needs to know that their guests will enjoy the experience as the visitors are their customers. As the tour leader might not be interested in experiencing the event because they are working rather than on a trip, there should be somewhere that they can relax while their tour customers enjoy themselves at the event.

The sales process demonstrates that there is much more to selling than just getting a consumer to hand over money in exchange for a product. A sales person will first listen to what a potential visitor or tour operator needs and then provide them with a solution. After all, both visitors and tour operators need events. At the heart of the marketing concept is the process of solving a problem for the consumer, and when the sales process is followed this is exactly what should happen.

In the case of approaching tour operators, the sales process begins with the first step of prospecting for the right decision-makers to contact. Tourism marketers can start the prospecting process by reviewing the names of any travel intermediaries or business groups with whom they have already had contact. In addition, hotel establishments in the city may be able to provide contact information for travel intermediaries with whom they have conducted business. Trade association directories and trade publications will also provide names of possible travel intermediaries who might be interested in having their customers enjoy the event.

Once a prospect has been identified, the tourism marketer must now research information about the customers it serves. The tourism marketer should also determine the geographic area the travel intermediary covers with their tours. Once this information is obtained, the tourism marketer should prioritize the list so that the most attractive prospects are contacted first.

Part of the sales process is to develop a personal relationship between the tourism organization and the decision-maker. The sales person should contact the decision-maker personally to make an appointment for either an informal meeting or a formal presentation. The organization may prepare a formal presentation with audiovisual and printed material that will be provided to a group of people; or the presentation may be a more informal meeting to provide initial information that the tourism marketer hopes will result in being asked back to discuss the proposal further. The purpose of either type of presentation is to provide only the most important information about how the event and its benefits fit with what the travel intermediary's customers desire.

The next step in the sales process is for the salesperson to handle any objections or issues raised by the decision-maker. If the organization has conducted prospecting correctly, the benefits the event offers should match the travel intermediary's needs. It is the sales person's responsibility to meet these objections with information that reassures decision-makers that they are making the right decision by considering the event as a potential destination. The sales person closes the presentation by providing information on how the event can be booked. Rather than just have a passive close, the sales person should be proactive and state exactly how to go about booking a group to visit the event, whom to contact and when the best time to book is.

Discussion questions

1. How are the traditional forms of promotion still useful?
2. What is the difference between paid, owned, earned and shared media?
3. Why has the communication model changed because of social media?
4. How does the AIDA model explain how promotional media motivates purchase?
5. Where can advertising be placed besides traditional media?
6. How has public relations changed because of the use of social media?
7. Why are sales incentives useful to motivate attendance?
8. What are some ways that all staff can be involved in personal selling?

Case

Using a second or third language to target visitors

It may be that you are not targeting an international visitor segment. Perhaps your event is new and small and you don't anticipate anyone traveling from another country for attendance. However international visitors may have traveled to your country for another reason. They are now online looking for additional activities. Attending your event may not require a high level of proficiency in your language, but learning about it will. Therefore, you may want to consider using more than one language in your promotion. Another reason for doing so is people within your targeted group that may not be native speakers. To promote in more than one language, the following needs to be considered.

- Which language? First you need to decide what language to use. If there is a large percentage of the local or regional population that speaks another language, this should be used. If you know that visitors from a specific country come to your area, even if not to your community, this language should also be used.
- What to translate? First you need to translate your website. Translation software can be used, but the resulting translation should be tested with native speakers to ensure that it is accurate and readable. It is particularly important that booking and payment instructions are clear. Also, consider SEO. If different terms are used to search for travel opportunities in other languages, they should be included on the translated website.
- Which sites to use? It may be too time-consuming to translate all marketing content posted online into other languages. Short postings about the event can be posted onto social media sites that are used in other countries. These can then have a link that will direct them to your translated website (DeGuide 2019).

Task: Decide into what languages your website should be translated and how the translation will be done.

Case

Now everyone does public relations

Public relations, or PR, previously was a specialized field where professionals communicated to the press what the company wanted the press to know. Social media has fundamentally changed the function and the profession. How? Check out these ways.

- Information speed: PR professionals use to spend a great deal of time writing up stories about the company, product or event that they then sent to journalists who then published them for the public. Now the time frame for stories is much shorter as a trending topic will reach many more people much more quickly. On Twitter, 6,000 exchanges happen every second.
- Crisis management: Because of the speed of communication, any bad news, even minor events, can be blown up out of proportion online. As a result, the organization must be hypervigilant in responding to any negative news. It will not disappear on its own.
- Customer service: Public relations has blurred with customer service. When a potential visitor has a concern about a product or event, they will share their concern with the organization, but also on social media. As a result, public relations must now also help maintain the integrity of the brand by constantly communicating positive and useful information (Lawlor 2019).

Task: How will your event organizers share news of the event so that a positive reputation is maintained?

Event plan: Use the information from this chapter to complete the first section of the event plan outline at the end of the book.

References

Buckley, Pete. 2019. "How Brands Can Thrive Despite the Squeeze on Consumers' Attention." *Marketing Week*. February 12, 2019. https://www.marketingweek.com/facebook-brands-thrive-squeeze-consumers-attention/. Accessed January 13, 2020.

DeGuide, Alison. 2019. "Four Ways to Promote Your Tours to an International Audience." *Regiondo*. December 15, 2019. https://pro.regiondo.com/tourism-promotion-ideas/. Accessed November 22, 2019.

Dermoudy, Amber. 2018. "Why Influencer Marketing is a Game Changer for Business." *Entrepreneur*. October 12, 2018. https://www.entrepreneur.com/article/321607. Accessed November 27, 2020.

Doerr, Patsy. 2018. "Four Ways Social Impact Will Affect Businesses in 2019." *Forbes*. January 14, 2018. https://www.forbes.com/sites/patsydoerr/2019/01/14/four-ways-social-impact-will-affect-businesses-in-2019/#57db06736e71. September January 12, 2020.

Lawlor, Jessica. 2019. "5 Ways Social Media Has Reshaped the PR Industry." *Ragan's PR Daily*. November 3, 2019. https://www.prdaily.com/5-ways-social-media-has-reshaped-the-pr-industry/. Accessed October 3, 2020.

Peek, Sean. 2020. "Social Media Integration: What It Is and How to Implement It." *Business News Daily*. January 22, 2020. https://www.businessnewsdaily.com/10525-social-media-integration.html. Accessed February 26, 2020.

Sen, Shahana, and Dawn Lerman. 2007. "Why Are You Telling Me This? An Examination into Negative Consumer Reviews on the Web." *Journal of Interactive Marketing* 21(4), 76–94.

Tama, Karina. 2019. "Finding the Sweet Spot with Traditional and Digital Marketing Examples." March 7, 2019. https://www.forbes.com/sites/forbescommunicationscouncil/2019/03/07/finding-the-sweet-spot-with-traditional-and-digital-marketing/?sh=1b6c0048129d. November 20, 2020.

Weisberg, Emily. 2019. "9 Sales Promotion Examples." *ThriveHive*. March 1, 2019. https://thrivehive.com/sales-promotion-examples/. Accessed August 18, 2019.

Wrobelewski, M.T. 2018. "The Advantages of Posters." *Small Business Chronicle*. November 5, 2018. https://smallbusiness.chron.com/advantages-posters-63269.html. Accessed August 19, 2019.

Chapter 11

Connecting with social media

Abstract

The organization will post information about the event on their own social media sites. The content posted should either educate or entertain. The purpose of the posting is to motivate potential visitors to post about the event on their own sites, creating earned media. If this information is then posted from one user to another it becomes shared media. This process amplifies the original promotional message. Social media can be used to move consumers from attention to action. Content marketing is not direct promotion. Its purpose is to engage the social media user so they will be interested in learning more about the event. Online users vary with only a portion becoming involved in sharing content. Showing evidence of a human personality online is effective in motivating users to share. Telling stories is more effective than merely presenting facts. To continually generate interest, new content must be posted on a regular basis. The type of content to be posted, whether visuals, text or video, should be maintained in a calendar. The organization should post the content on social media sites their targeted visitors use. Success should be measured by analyzing reach, volume, engagement and conversion of social media users.

Earned and shared media strategy

Media can be categorized as paid, owned, earned and shared. The purpose of paid media is to build awareness of the event and attract visitors to the organization's owned media. Paid media may be traditional print media used by tourist organizations including ads, brochures and posters and also include broadcast forms such as TV and radio ads. Now paid media also includes digital social media ads.

Owned media would include all social media sites that are controlled by the organization. These might be sites dedicated to the organization or Facebook and other social media networking sites developed specifically for the event. The tourism and hospitality organizations could also have their own Instagram and Pinterest accounts if they feel that their potential visitors use these when searching for information. The social media used depends on what types of sites their potential visitors use. The organization would also open accounts on these sites because it is here that they are most likely to be found by potential visitors. If the organization is going to create promotional videos about the event, then a YouTube or other video-sharing channel should be considered.

Blogging and microblogging or tweeting are also a form of owned media as it is communication controlled by the organization. Even if the organization is resending a blog or tweet sent by someone else, the information that is sent is still in the organization's control as they have the choice of what to resend. What is unique about owned media is that the organization controls the message. Therefore it is a direct link of information to the targeted potential visitor.

Earned media strategy

The purpose of using owned media to promote the event is to motivate potential visitors to create earned media by communicating online about their interest in visiting the event. Earned media is the mention of the organization and the event on social media sites not controlled by the organization. In order to generate earned media, the organization can use content marketing. This is the placement of information on owned media that will either educate or entertain the social media user.

Earned media is a direct response to information that was posted by the organization. Something that was posted either prompted the reader or viewer to request more information. This might be before the event with a response that includes questions on pricing, the venue or the activities that will occur. Another type of response could be a response that is simply supportive of the event. A reader might respond with enthusiasm that they will be attending. A third type of response might be negative. In this case the respondent might feel that the event activities are inappropriate or the pricing is too high. All types of messages, but especially negative comments, should receive a response from the organizations. A study of hotel reviews posted online found that when hotels made a practice of always responding to negative reviews, their positive reviews increased by 12 percent (Proserpio and Giorgos 2018).

The organization will welcome all types of response. When social media is used to answer questions about the event, the information in the response is then also provided to other people on the site. These social media users may also have had the same question but might not have asked it. Positive remarks from people excited about the event should be publicly thanked, generating even more excitement. Finally, negative comments can be addressed by providing more information as to the rationale behind the pricing or activity choices.

Earned media becomes shared media when the initial information by the organization is shared by a reader with others in their own social groups or sites. This amplifies the marketing message to new recipients that may not have been reached with the original message. Examples of shared media include recipients of tweets then retweeting the message to others. It can also include sharing Facebook postings on the recipients' own social networking sites. Shared media is effective because it broadens the reach of the marketing message. With each sharing, this reach expands.

Shared media strategy

The organization needs to consider their overall strategy for using social media to generate shared media. Posting for posting's sake is not the reason for having owned media sites. If there aren't specific goals on what it is hoped will be achieved by posting, there will be no way to justify the time that was spent.

Social media is not free. The costs include the time spent preparing content and then posting. It also includes the time that is spent reviewing and responding to postings from the public. It is sometimes thought that this work can be done by a volunteer or intern as it is easy to find someone who enjoys being on social media. While posting information is an easy task, a volunteer or intern will not be familiar with the type of information that needs to be conveyed and also the style in which this should be done. They will also not be familiar with the words and visuals that will enhance and reinforce the branded image of the event. Instead, someone inside the organization should be put in charge of social media. If outside experts are hired, they will need to be closely supervised to ensure that all information posted is appropriate.

The first goal of any social media strategy is to gain awareness of the event. However, simply providing information alone will not motivate the social media user to take action. One way to know if the use of social media is effective is if people click and purchase tickets on the site. If it is not a ticketed event, then social media should be used to gauge people's intent to attend in some other way. This could be by noting if people are requesting additional information or posting online that they plan on attending. If the event is free, there still may be the need to sell bookings for lodging, which can then be tracked. While the main event may be free, other activities, such as tours or beverage packages, might be sold and tracked.

Social media and the AIDA model

Social media is an excellent means of moving people from awareness, to interest, desire and finally action (Third 2019). To do so requires more than random posting. People often start their searching for events on a search engine such as Google. If they are considering a trip, they aren't searching for a specific event but rather general information using the name of the destination or type of event. The organization needs to ensure that information on their event will appear in search engine results when these types of searches are made. This means that the keywords that are used in the description of the event are the correct ones. This can be discovered by conducting a search to see what words bring up competing events. When the potential visitor sees the results from a generalized search, the event link creates awareness. They will then hopefully click on the link and be brought to the event website.

Once the potential visitor is on the event website, the organization has only seconds to develop interest in possible attendance. To do so the company must understand why they are coming to the site and what information they need. To hold their interest, this information must be written in an engaging manner using exciting words and visuals. These are designed to create desire so that people stay on the site long enough to learn of the benefits that the event provides. One way to create desire online is to let the consumer experience the product first hand. This can be done through sneak peaks of the entertainment and activities.

Finally, social media will help the potential visitor take action by requesting information or buying tickets. The website or other social media site must have a clear and easy call to action. Where and when the event is taking place and how tickets can be purchased must be clearly explained. This step can be encouraged by offering discounts or small gifts for immediately taking action.

Content marketing purpose

Content marketing is the posting of information that either educates or entertains the consumer. It is not a promotional message and is not designed to motivate immediate purchase. The purpose of content marketing is to engage the potential visitor by posting information on the organization's website or social media site that is useful or entertaining. It is hoped that the reader or viewer will share the information with others, seek out more information about the event or contact the organization directly. Even if they take none of these steps, if they find the information posted of interest they are more likely to return to the site for more postings.

If the potential visitor seeks out more information and learns the event has the benefits they desire, they will then promote the event to others. Besides attracting potential visitors with content of interest, the online conversations will help the organization to learn more about their visitors' desires or concerns and be able to improve the event offerings.

Just as with paid media such as print ads, billboards and brochures, the aim of content marketing is to capture the attention of the targeted potential visitor as quickly as possible. This need to capture attention in seconds means that if the content doesn't immediately attract, the reader moves on. While social media users may not be conscious of the fact, readers who are viewing an online site are asking whether the content has any meaning for them. If the first few words or the image do not convey any reason why the reader should stop, they will move on.

The content on the site might engage a social media user because it has an emotional connection to a past or present event portrayed by the words or pictures. It might also engage attention as it solves a problem of what to do on an upcoming holiday. The potential visitor browsing online will only stop on the social media site if the content either evokes an emotion or answers their specific question. If it does so, the potential visitor will then stay long enough to read or view content, whether the written word, image or video. When these sufficiently convince consumers that the event will provide them with the desired benefits, they will then move forward in the purchase process.

While some social media users may only frequent one site, most use more than one site. The use of social media is almost universal but the way that people use social media differs (Majors 2018). Types of users include relationship-builders who use social media the way it was originally intended, which is to stay connected with friends and family. They will use social media to share their trip plans before, during and after the event with people they know. Rather than use social media to connect with others, a category of users will use sites to send messages about themselves. For these users, posting information on their trip is a way to enhance their own image. They record their trip day by day and, for some, hour by hour, and then post online. Finally, there are the people-watchers of social media. They are online looking and reading about trips and events but rarely post or even like.

Building online relationships

If the organization wants to build a relationship with the public using content marketing, they will need to show their human side (Balkhi 2019). This is particularly effective for organizations developing events because socialization is part of the event benefit. People who attend events want to meet with others. It is natural that they will also want to know more about the people organizing the event. To do so involves the organization sharing appropriate personal information. Posting photos of staff members busy organizing the event or at the venue site making preparations can make the organization real in a way that only using a blog posting cannot. Having fun online by posting humorous stories or comics, particularly if they poke fun at the organization, can help people relate. Even sharing mistakes can help personalize the organization if they are shared with humility and a commitment that the mistake will not be made again.

Posting appropriate content

Rather than being designed to simply sell a product, the information contained in content marketing must either educate or entertain. The information it shares might be about the event, but it is more likely to be about the organization and the staff involved in creating the event. In addition, the content will share news stories that the potential visitor might find to be of interest. In fact, rather than promote its own event, it can share information on other events that might be of interest to its visitors. The other purpose of content is to solve a problem for the consumer. There is a reason that the words "how to" are one of the most frequently used online search terms. Therefore, by providing content that solves a problem, such as what items to bring along to a festival, the organization engages the interest of the potential visitor without trying to sell a ticket.

A relevant issue for marketers using social media is how much of the content should directly promote the product. After all, revenue is only received when someone attends. This concern has become outdated as consumers no longer draw a sharp distinction between a brand, a product and the owners of the company. All content is in some way promotional if it draws attention to your organization and event. The distinction is that content marketing promotes indirectly.

Using stories in content marketing

Stories are an effective way of gaining the attention of social media users. As humans, our brains are programmed to respond to stories. Long before humans had written language, all information that was vital for survival needed to be imparted orally. Facts are better remembered if they are included in stories that provoke emotion.

Stories can be particularly effective in promoting events. As the event product is intangible and what is being purchased cannot be experienced before purchase, simple facts about the event might not motivate purchase. Stories start with the idea for the main character. The beginning of the story introduces the character, which should be reflective of the visitor segment being targeted. This could be a bored young man with nothing to do on the weekend or a harried mother who needs a break.

The middle of the story will revolve around a conflict and its resolution. Perhaps the lonely young man attends the event where he meets a new best friend who shares a common interest. Perhaps the mother now again enjoys being with her family because of attending. In both cases the benefits of attending are not simply given as a list of facts but told through stories. At the end of the story the conflict is resolved by attending an event. The beginning, middle and end of the story do not need to be in this order. To engage the viewer's attention, the story could start with the conflict and then introduce the character and then the resolution.

Videos are an excellent way to communicate these stories. They do not need to be professionally produced to be effective. In fact, a more authentic look may be more attractive to the targeted visitor. The video can even show animated characters. The video will show people acting out the story or it can be told in a first-person narrative. The emotions that are triggered can be humor or empathy at the predicament faced by the video character. What motivates attendance is how attending the event is the resolution to the conflict.

Content marketing process

One of the challenges of content marketing is how to stay current with the posting. There are some simple steps that can help with making the process easier to maintain. First, the organization should decide on broad themes for the content that will be provided. The organization may decide to focus on sharing community news or news about a specific entertainer that will be appearing. Another theme might be news about a specific historical event that is the focus of the event. Choosing a theme will encourage readers to return for similar stories, opinions or ideas.

These returning readers will want fresh content when they return to the site. Developing a calendar, and even a time of day, when each piece of content will be uploaded will ensure that it gets done even on busy days. While a simple calendar can be used to list the frequency with which content needs to be posted, an editorial calendar determines what type of content will be provided. For example, one day may focus on local events while another day of the week will focus on new event activities. Developing templates for regular editorial features will speed up the process of content writing. These might be highlights of the week, interview questions and other standard content.

The content that will be used to meet the goal might be visuals, video or text. Other general guidelines when providing content include using multimedia whenever possible as people are drawn to images. In addition, adding personal opinions when sharing news stories adds to the interest. If stuck for a subject on which to write, following up on comments made on previous postings can provide a topic.

Steps in the process

The content marketing process involves planning, purpose, distribution, measurement and promotion. Planning includes deciding on the goals for content marketing. The goal might be simply to grow awareness or it might be to sell a specific number of tickets. The goal will determine the type of content that is going to be produced. Writing a goal that is challenging and yet achievable can be difficult. There are a number of models that can be used when writing goals. The SMART model is one of the most widely known. This model states that successful goals are specific, measurable, attainable, relevant and time-bound. The goal must give specific information as to what is to be achieved, such as selling tickets. The goal should also include a quantifiable factor that can be measured. This might be 30 percent of tickets will be presold before the event. This quantifiable goal should be realistic so that it can be attained. The goal should also be relevant to the overall strategy of the organization. For example, if the strategy of the organization is to increase online sales of event souvenirs, the goal should not be about promoting the food and beverages that will be at the event. Finally, for any goal to be successful specific dates for achieving each step must be given.

The purpose of the content should be consistent. For example, the purpose of the content might be to help the social media user prepare for the event or assist in some other way. The posting could explain what to bring to the event to make it more enjoyable. It could also share some of the entertainment so that the user can preview it and decide how to structure their limited time at the event. If there are activities that will be held at the event, the purpose of the content could be to describe how these activities can also be enjoyed at home. For example, if an activity such as pet photography is part of the event, the content could teach the user how to take better photos of their own pets. If lessons in textile dyeing will be part of the event, a video can be shared on how this can be done at home. This way, the content benefits the social media user even if they don't attend.

Distribution refers to the type of content that will be provided, along with where it will be posted. Blogs are commonly used for content marketing, but they do require the social media user to pause and read. Because this takes effort on the part of the user, videos and podcasts are becoming a more popular method of content marketing. A video requires minimal effort on the part of the user and is more easily made entertaining. An even easier way to provide information is using an infographic. When an event has lots of different activities and entertainment, an infographic can present the schedule for everything at a glance.

Social media sites change rapidly. What was once popular with a specific visitor segment may now be used by a different population or may not be used at all. The popularity of social media sites also varies by country. It will take some research to determine what are the best sites for distribution of the content. Of course, the first place the content should be posted is on the event's own website. Next would be a popular networking site such as Facebook. Video-sharing sites such as YouTube or Vimeo should be used. Twitter can also be used for sharing content. Image-sharing sites such as Instagram and Pinterest should also be considered.

Measurement would have to be done to see if the content was being viewed and also if the viewing of the content led to meeting the goals. If not, changes to the content need to be considered. If content is not being noticed online, promotion of the content may be needed. Since staff time is spent on creating content, the organization should not simply hope that it is noticed. This is particularly true if the content is only posted on the organization's website. While current customers will probably see and may read the content, it is less likely that potential visitors will notice. Therefore, the organization may decide to use paid promotion to attract readers. This can be done by buying ads on social networking sites. This can be a particularly effective method of promotion for small and medium-sized organizations. Social media ads can be targeted at groups based on interests, geography, or both. Content can also be shared by sending promoted tweets. While the organization will tweet links to their current followers, these will not include prospects. Therefore, paying to be able to tweet to a group of people who may be potential customers may be worth the cost.

Steps in the content marketing process

- Planning: Deciding on goals to be achieved through content.
- Creating: Writing or videoing content of interest.
- Distributing: Posting on a regular basis on select social media sites.
- Promoting: Using paid media to promote content.

Assessing social media effectiveness

The methods for creating an effective social media strategy that will connect organizations with consumers continues to evolve. In reality, there may not be a single social media strategy that works for all types of businesses and organizations. However, almost all strategies recommend that the organization first connect with the public by having its own social media sites. However, having the sites is the easy part of the model. The challenge will be in using the sites effectively.

There are four steps in creating a social media strategy (Sharma 2019). The first is the same as with any strategy, which is to define the organization's goals. The goal might be to simply attract more visitors to the site. However this does not on its own create additional revenue. Other goals might be to increase sales from returning visitors or to reach new visitors, both of which would increase attendance and revenue. If there is a new visitor segment that is being targeted, their social media preferences must be understood. The next choice would be to decide which social media sites should be used as part of the strategy. The last step is then to analyze the results in either increased number of visitors, increased sales, or both.

Types of metrics

There are numerous ways that online activity can be measured. When analyzing the use of social media to promote an event's reach, volume, engagement and conversion should be analyzed. Reach is a measure of how many people have seen the content on social media. Content about the event will have been posted on the organization's own website and other social media sites. This analysis will inform the organization of which sites attracted the most users. There are three types of reach that can be measured. Organic reach is how many people have seen the posting. Viral reach is when someone shares the posting with others. Promoted reach is when the posting appears in a newsfeed where it will be seen by someone not on the organization's social media. This type of reach can be broadened through the use of promoted posts. If a posting about the event, such as best time to buy discounted tickets or the name of an entertainer, proves popular, the organization will want it to be seen by more people. If the decision is made to pay to have the post appear in a news feed on other social media sites, the question remains of what sites to target. Social media sites can provide this information by analyzing the organization's own users and then finding a site that attracts a similar audience.

The next metric to analyze would be volume. All product brands are talked about online. Of course, well-known and popular events will be included in more conversations. More important than only knowing the number of people discussing the event is how it is comparing with people talking about competing events in posts and messages. Volume is increased when the event name is mentioned on other social media sites. These are more difficult to assess on social media without specialized software. Hashtags for an event are a quick and easy way for the public to converse online. The number of times the event hashtags are used are an indication of volume and can be measured. If it is found that there is insufficient volume, other marketing activities must be expanded to build awareness.

A third metric to follow is engagement. Volume and reach measure if the public is aware of the event. Engagement measures if they are expressing interest through action. Measures of engagement such as likes and shares means that social media users find the postings of value. Tweets and retweets do the same. More important is an increase of followers of the event. These followers are interested in learning more and are moving closer to becoming actual visitors. Ways to increase engagement include running online contests, surveys of interest and using videos.

A final metric is the most important, and that is conversion. This is when the social media user moves from awareness to action. If tickets are purchased online, this is the surest way of measuring intent to attend. However, if the event does not require ticketing, conversion becomes more difficult to measure. Intent to attend can also be measured by conversions such as sending for more information about the event. Posting questions on a chatbot would be another measure of conversation. Simply asking users of social media to post their intention to attend could be another.

Social media analysis

- Reach: Number of people who have seen content.
- Volume: People mentioning event online.
- Engagement: Taking action to learn more.
- Conversion: Purchase.

Increasing social media metrics

If the social media metrics are not as positive as would be liked, there are steps the organization can use to increase their numbers. The first issue to address is the target keywords that are contained in social media content postings. It is these key words that will determine if the content appears in search engine results. It may be that the posted content is not being found when potential visitors do online searches because the wrong words are being used. To gain the attention of their targeted audience who are currently unaware of the event, the organization needs to know what they are searching for online. This might be weekend getaways, fun at the beach, historic sites, cheap events or family-friendly hotels. If the event meets these criteria, then the exact same words need to be in the posting so that they will be found by the search engine. This will take research and then some experimentation before the right words are found.

Just collecting data on social media metrics alone is not helpful. What will be useful for the organization is determining how to use the data to connect with more potential visitors by providing the desired information on the right social media sties (Vaccaro, Mager, Groff and Bolante 2019). Social media metrics will help the organization understand if the social media user is finding that the posting provides value. Purely promotional postings asking people to attend will be ignored. Instead the posting must provide information on how it is solving a problem held by members of the targeted visitor segment. This could range from how to party all night to having fun at a substance-free event. Social media metrics will help the organization understand how the information posted about their event meets the needs of their unique targeted audience.

Response time

A final aspect of social media metrics is the level of customer service that is being provided. The goal of a social media strategy is to move the targeted visitor segment from attention to action. This should result in members of the targeted visitor segment contacting the organization with questions, for more information, or making a ticket purchase. Response time is how fast the organization gets back to the social media user requesting information. Members of the public have become very demanding on a quick, almost immediate, response time.

Many people are now preferring to contact companies via social media rather than phone or email. They want to avoid phone calls because they anticipate a lengthy wait time on hold. Even when the phone is answered they then often encounter confusing menu options. While these are designed to speed enquires to the right person who can provide assistance, they are time-consuming for the caller. People do not want to leave a voice message with an organization and wait for a return phone call that will interrupt their day. Also, many busy people will not respond to a phone call unless they know the caller. Emails take time to compose and the response when it arrives may be lost in the stream of emails that are received.

For these reasons, people now want to connect with companies on social media sites. A majority of respondents expect a response to an inquiry posted on social media the same day (Barnhart 2020). On a platform such as Twitter they expect a response within the hour. If the organization does not respond, they are likely to both complain online about the delay and then contact a competitor. If a number of different social media sites are being used, it can be difficult to ensure that all inquiries receive a response. To help with responding on time, there are software tools that can be used that channel all enquiries into a single space. This ensures response consistency. It will also allow the person responsible for responding to save the answers to repeatedly asked questions, speeding up response time.

The use of chatbots is no longer only a tool for large businesses. Even small organizations can set up a chatbot that will answer routine questions. The responses that are programed should be personalized and match the personality of the organization. People should always be given the option of not using a chatbot as they are sometimes found to be annoying.

Discussion questions

1. What is the purpose of posting event information on organization controlled media sites?
2. What is the difference between earned media and shared media?
3. How does social media amplify the original promotional message?
4. Why should content marketing be written to show a personality?
5. What kind of stories about an upcoming event could be shared online?
6. What types of content can be posted online?
7. How can a content calendar be helpful when conducting content marketing?
8. How should the success of content marketing be analyzed?

Potential visitors want to know everything

Of course, you are posting on all your social media sites what your event is about, where it is taking place and when it is happening. But how many times can you post this same information before it becomes boring? Content marketing is providing the more in-depth information that your visitors need, even before they ask. This is your chance to share unique places and experiences that social media users don't even know exist so they can't search for them. These are the experiences that will help motivate a visit because they can then be shared online. The content can become a local travel guide supplied in bite-sized pieces. You can share information on the following.

- Restaurants: Provide information on different types of local restaurants. It is even better if you include a photo of their staff showing off menu items.
- Lodging: Give a unique take on the various lodging choices by including a greeting by the staff describing why their place is best.
- Transportation: Post information on the options on how to get to the destination. Include links to transport maps and parking lots.
- Videos: Take short videos of the local area that include local residents sharing why they feel visitors should come to the event.
- History: Not everyone loves history, but everyone loves something unique. Tell them about a remarkable resident or place that is unique to the destination.
- Share: When people respond to your content, respond, and the communication can be the subject for another content marketing post (Harris 2018).

Task: List ten posting ideas for your event content marketing.

Social media isn't free

Social media is essential when marketing a service such as an event. Potential visitors want to be reassured that what they will experience will meet their needs. They need to see the marketing message but they will also use social media to research the event. Potential visitors don't only need information from the organization, they want information posted by other visitors. Only social media can provide this type of communication.

There is a misconception that using social media for promotion is free. All that is necessary is to come up with great ideas to market your event or destination and then post. However, there are costs involved that will affect both your staffing and budgeting.

- Staff: Promotional ideas must be created. This takes imagination in developing ideas that communicate the brand to motivate attendance. Not everyone will have these skills. Either current employees will need to be provided with training or new staff will need to be hired.
- Time: Once content is posted, it must be monitored. Potential visitors are highly influenced by the opinions of others who have attended in the past. Someone in the organization must be allotted time to monitor social media and respond to both positive and negative comments.
- Budget: Social media costs money to develop and host the needed social media sites. The sites must be designed to reflect the event brand. If the organization's own staff does not have the ability, skilled professionals will need to be hired. In addition, social media ads will need to be purchased (Chen 2019).

Task: Decide who on your staff will be responsible for social marketing strategy implementation and create a budget line for ad placement.

Event plan: Use the information from this chapter to complete the first section of the event plan outline at the end of the book.

References

Balkhi, Syed. 2019. "5 Things You Can Do to 'Humanize' Your Brand." *Entrepreneur.* January 7, 2019. https://www.entrepreneur.com/article/325370. Accessed November 7, 2020.

Barnhart, Brent. 2020. "Why You Need to Speed Up Your Social Media Response Time (and How)." *Sprout Social.* June 24, 2020. https://sproutsocial.com/insights/social-media-response-time/. Accessed November 30, 2020.

Chen, Jenn. 2019. "How to Set Up a Social Media for Travel Marketing Strategy." *SproutSocial.* December 17, 2019. https://sproutsocial.com/insights/social-media-for-travel/. Accessed September 12, 2020.

Harris, Jodi. 2018. "How to Take Your Travel Content on a Better Trip." *Content Marketing Institute.* June 22, 2018. https://contentmarketinginstitute.com/2018/06/travel-content/. Accessed December 23, 2020.

Majors, Tim. 2018. "The 4 Types of Social Media Users." *Uptick.* March 22 2018. https://uptickmarketing.com/4-types-social-media-users/. Accessed February 13, 2020.

Proserpio, Davide, and Giorgos Zervas. 2018. "Study: Replying to Customer Reviews Results in Better Ratings." *Harvard Business Review.* February 14, 2018. https://hbr.org/2018/02/study-replying-to-customer-reviews-results-in-better-ratings. Accessed on October 22, 2020.

Sharma, Gauray. 2019. "4 Steps for Creating a Social Media Strategy [Infographic]." *Social Media Today.* July 15, 2019. https://www.socialmediatoday.com/news/4-steps-for-creating-a-solid-social-media-strategy-infographic/558752/. Accessed August 30, 2020.

Third, Jake. 2019. "How to Apply the AIDA Model to Digital Marketing." *Hallam.* November 11, 2019. https://www.hallaminternet.com/apply-aida-model-digital-marketing/. Accessed March 27, 2020.

Vaccaro, Angel, Scott Mager, Natalie Groff, and Alex Bolante. 2019. "Beyond Marketing: Experience Reimagined." February 26, 2019. https://deloitte.wsj.com/cmo/2019/02/26/beyond-marketing-experience-reimagined/. Accessed November 1, 2020.

Chapter 12

Assessing event success

Abstract

After the event has ended there will still be administrative, physical and evaluative responsibilities to complete. Administrative responsibilities include closing down financial accounts and evaluating the success of the promotional campaigns. Physical tasks include clean-up and trash removal. Evaluative work involves determining if goals were met, including the decision as to whether the event should be held again. Visitor satisfaction can be determined through observation and noting what activities are popular. A survey can be given after the event to gain knowledge. Personal interviews are helpful in providing ideas for improvement. The budget needs to be analyzed to see if the financial goals set for the event were met. The economic impact of the event on the business community should be assessed. Visitor numbers should be calculated and then analyzed to see if the targeted visitor segment attended. The economic impact of the event will be of interest to the community. This would include the increase in sales of local merchants. Sponsors should be visited after the event to determine if their goals were met and to gather information for the future.

Closing the event down

After the last visitor has left the event, there is still work for the staff to perform. There are tasks that are administrative involving financial record-keeping and post-event marketing. Physical tasks involve clean-up and storage. The evaluative tasks would include an assessment of whether the event objectives were met. This assessment can then be split into front-end and back-end (Byvalkevych 2019). The front end involves an assessment of the visitor experience. The back end would assess how the organization and staff implemented the event components that created the experience.

Administrative tasks

Administrative responsibilities include the bookkeeping function of closing the financial accounts. While deposits may have been paid, the final bill for items such as catering, tent rentals and sanitation services may not be due until after the event is completed. With post-event exhaustion, this final step can be overlooked. Someone should be assigned the task of not only making the payments but appropriately recording the expenses in the accounts. Likewise, any revenue due to the organization because of sponsorships or payments from vendors needs to be collected before the accounting function is complete. The longer collecting bills is ignored, the more difficult it will become to get paid. Once the accounts are completed, a comparison of projected versus actual visitor and revenue numbers will be evaluated. The finances of larger events will be more challenging to assess because of the number of different revenue sources.

There will also be final marketing responsibilities such as posting of post-event photos on social media sites. Press releases should be sent to local media outlets describing the success of the event. Finally, thanks should be sent to all organizations and businesses that have supported the event through financial contributions, providing volunteers or media coverage. Their enthusiastic participation will again be needed when the next event is planned.

Physical tasks

The most important physical tasks are cleaning up and packing up after the event. The reputation that the event has with the community will depend on ensuring that it leaves no lasting negative effects. The visitors and vendors will leave the site but the trash that remains will need to be removed. For a small event this might be handled by volunteers with trash bags and a truck to haul the bags away. For large events, a trash removal service provider may be needed. Food and other product vendors may have brought their own tables and tents from which to display and sell. They need to be given a deadline for when this equipment needs to be removed.

Once the trash is removed, any product and equipment that belong to the sponsoring organizations need to be boxed and stored. This will include any printed material, signage and furniture. Sound and lighting equipment will also need to be packed and put back in storage or returned to from where it was rented. Finally, any large equipment such as sanitation, stages and seating need to be removed. If the event was outdoors in a public place, any damage to lawns and other landscaping needs to be repaired.

Assessment process

Finally, the task of evaluating and reporting the success of the event needs to be handled. The purpose of evaluation is to help improve future events. For a small event, this might involve simply asking event staff what successes they observed and also what problems they encountered during the event. For most events, a more formal assessment process is needed.

After the event is over and all the physical aspects have been cleared from the site, an evaluation of the management of the event can begin. This evaluation can identify management problems so that they do not occur the next time the event is held (Wong 2019). For example, a shortage of transportation may have left visitors stranded at the site after it closed. It is then known that more transportation options need to be considered for the next event. Staff evaluation also needs to be conducted. This will assess if the people working at the event were able to meet visitor needs in a friendly and efficient manner. It will also assess if the management in charge of the event were able to successfully handle any problems that occurred. The purpose of this assessment is not to place blame but rather to ensure that employee skills are better matched to responsibilities for the next event.

The question of whether the event provided the benefits desired by visitors also needs to be answered. Since an event is a package of activities and products, it may be necessary to evaluate each separately. First, there may be activities that went brilliantly and should be performed exactly the same at the next event. There is no reason to expend valuable resources changing an activity when the visitors were pleased. There may be a second group of activities that went well but need some improvement. Perhaps the lines at certain activities were long and next time more seating space is needed. The third group would be activities that had problems. Perhaps it is found that the food provided was not of interest to visitors. This can be fixed for the next event by having different options. Finally, some activities with problems should not be repeated. If there was no interest in expensive entertainment, there is no reason to spend the same amount of money at the next event.

There are numerous ways evaluation can be conducted. Which method should be used depends on the goals that were set during the planning process. One of the possible goals might have been the number of visitors who attended. This is easily evaluated by comparing actual with projected visitors. It might also have been the total revenue produced, which is also easy to assess using variance analysis. Some goals, such as improved destination reputation, will be harder to assess. This type of assessment might take time, such as looking to see if visitor numbers increase in the future or to see if event visitors return.

Types of tasks

- Administrative: Depositing revenue, paying bills, posting social media.
- Physical: Trash removal, return of equipment, material storage for next event.
- Assessment: Management, staff, visitors, sponsors.

Event life span

Events, just like products, have a life span. The product life cycle starts with introduction and moves on to a period of growth and then maturity. After these stages comes a natural stage of decline. At this point the organization must decide whether to revitalize the event or end its production.

When a new event is introduced, revenue may not be immediate but expenses will be. Launching a new product of any type, including events, will require funding for the initial development. For events this will include down payments for venues and entertainment. It will also include marketing expenses. There will be revenue from early ticket sales but they will not be enough to offset expenses. As a result, there will be a need for initial funding. The product or event then goes into a stage of growth. For repeat events this might not be until the second or even third time the event is held. The positive response from the first event will result in reviews and postings causing attendance to grow in the future. After a while, the event will move to maturity. This is when visitor numbers stabilize. The organization is confident that they can expect a certain number of visitors each time the event is held but not continued growth in visitor numbers. Growth does not go up indefinitely as there is a limit on the number of people within the target market that can be attracted to attend.

The organization would be satisfied if this current level continued year after year but this will not happen. All products eventually enter a period of decline. This can happen for several reasons. It might be that the very success of the event has inspired other communities to offer similar events that cause a loss of visitors. The reason for the decline may be internal to the organization; for example, the loss of a venue that was offered without cost so a less desirable venue had to be used. The decline could happen because those who created the event have moved on to other jobs and new employees are not as interested in investing the required funds and effort.

A common reason for the decline in an event is that the external environment has changed causing potential visitors to desire different benefits. Entertainment that was once popular is no longer so. Trends such as an interest in a particular culture has declined. Technology that was once considered cutting edge is now commonplace. It might be a social reason as people's awareness of environmental effects of the event are the cause of a decline in attendance. It might also be an economic reason, as during a period of economic decline potential visitors may not be able to afford the cost.

When an event enters a period of decline in visitor number there might not be a simple solution. However, if the decline is ignored, financial losses will continue to increase, which will cause the funds needed to be taken from other programs. Instead, an event in decline needs to be evaluated as to whether it can be changed to increase its popularity. Each component of the event needs to be evaluated to see if it can be improved or should be eliminated. It might be found that the needed changes will be too expensive or it might be found that the event cannot be updated to meet current visitor desires.

It is not a failure to end a long-running event if it can no longer be sustained. Instead, the success of the event over the years should be celebrated. The organization is then freed up to explore new event ideas that will draw in visitors.

Event visitor assessment

Part of the planning for a tourism event should be considering how to assess the effectiveness in meeting the original goals. Some of the aspects that will need to be evaluated are easier to calculate than others. The number of tickets sold and the revenue produced are simple quantitative measures, where the results can be compared with what was projected. More difficult to ascertain is the economic benefit that resulted from the event. The most difficult to assess would be the changed or enhanced image of the community.

Assessment by observation

A simple and inexpensive method for assessing the success of an event is to use observation research. Obtaining information with verbal questions about past behavior is difficult. For example, it may be difficult to ask families, when they are leaving an event, which activity they enjoyed most. First, the family may have hungry and tired children and not be interested in answering questions. Second, they simply may not remember at that time. After they are home, they are unlikely to take the time to respond to a survey because they are busy with family and work. However, if visitors are observed at the event, the organization will be able to determine which attractions families stop to enjoy, and which attractions they pass by.

One type of observation is where the researcher is a "complete observer" and acts as a "fly-on-the-wall." Here observers remove themselves from the scene to record what they observe from a distance. For example, the observer would simply watch families from a distance at a music fest to determine what activities they engaged in the most. Another type is participant observation. For example, if researchers really want to know how people feel about the city's guided walking tours, they can join one as a participant. This allows them not only to observe the visitors conduct – are they hurried, or bored? – but also to overhear both positive and negative comments.

Event managers will still need to put some time into planning the structure of the research when using observation. For the research findings to be useful, the issue of where, when and whom to observe must be considered. For example, when observing tours, it should be remembered that the demographic and psychographic characteristics of participants will vary based on the time and type of the tour. Therefore, when observing guided tours, more than one should be chosen and, if possible, a sample consisting of tours with different tour guides should be observed.

When all observations are completed the notes will then be analyzed for themes or problems that were common to most observations. The researcher will then compile this analysis into a report of what has been observed. For example, the researcher might have found that on all walking tours, most tourists' attention seemed to wander after about 40 minutes. Another observation might be that at the arts fest, children and parents quickly became frustrated if they had to wait for more than ten minutes for an activity to start. This information is critical in then planning the next event so as to maximize the benefits that visitors receive.

Assessment by social media

Social media provides opportunities for conducting research on event satisfaction. This type of research does not provide quantifiable information as it is difficult to count retweets, shares and likes across more than one platform. It is also impossible to determine the demographic characteristics and geographic location of those who are taking these actions online. However, social media marketing research can still be used to gain insight into visitor satisfaction with past events. First, online reviews of the event, lodgings and other businesses visited can tell whether expectations have been met. Social networking sites discussions can be followed about an event to determine what activities are recommended and which are disappointing visitors. Such types of research are still being developed because new forms of social media are always being introduced.

Assessment by survey

While it is common practice to send out surveys via email or by posting on social media there are advantages when an organization chooses to have staff personally administer the survey questions. This could be done as visitors are leaving the event, to learn whether the event met their expectations by asking a few simple questions. This might be as simple as asking what they liked best, what they liked least and suggestions for improvement. With this survey process, someone will ask the questions verbally and then record the answers. A major advantage of this method is that participants can ask for clarification of any difficult or confusing questions. Even simple survey questions such as, "How often have you attended the event?" may prompt questions. For example, the visitor might ask if this includes the current occasion or a time years ago. Without the researcher's explanation the visitor will have to guess whether these occasions should be counted as "visits."

Survey completion is always an issue. Having a staff member present to encourage visitors to answer all the questions helps completion. Even the most motivated past visitors starting an online survey in their own homes may then get interrupted by a phone call or family member. Unfortunately, when this happens there is no guarantee that they will return to complete the form. A staff-administered survey eliminates these distractions and ensures the form is completed. With a self-administered survey, participants may completely skip questions they find sensitive or difficult to answer and yet these might be the answers most needed by the organization. A staff-assisted survey allows the encouragement of event visitors to not skip these questions.

A final advantage of using staff-assisted surveying is when working with disenfranchised groups. Members of these groups may feel that they have no stake in the decision-making process and not be motivated to participate. Or, the members may not have the language skills or cultural knowledge to complete a survey that is sent to them. Whether the reluctance to participate is from a feeling of being outside the system or from a lack of understanding of the process, it may take the persuasive skills of the staff member before such visitors will cooperate and complete the survey.

Assessment by interviews

There has been an emphasis on collecting and analyzing a large quantity of data to help in decision-making. This trend to what is called big data can be useful. However, personal interviewing of visitors has the advantage of face-to-face contact that can uncover the complex purchase motivations that data alone cannot provide (McDonald 2018). Personal interviewing encourages participation because it allows the researcher to explain the purpose of the research and how the results will be used.

Personal surveying can be conducted where it is most convenient for the individuals who meet the participant profile are located. For example, the organization may wish to learn more about the visit experience from families, single visitors or members of a specific age group. If the organization wishes to survey families, they may decide to do so at the event near where family activities are occurring. If young women and men are the targeted population, the organization may conduct the surveys where they may naturally congregate, such as near entertainment. When asking visitors to participate in an interview, the organization has an advantage, as the research will be used for the social benefit of improving the event and not just to sell a product. When at the location where the interview will be conducted, the researcher must first ascertain that the potential visitor meets the profile characteristics. The researcher may first need to ask the potential participant screening questions to see if they fit the demographic, geographic and psychographic participant profile.

When conducting personal interviews, the researcher can use visual prompts that can assist the participant in answering the question. For example, if the organization wishes to learn more about the effectiveness of the event promotional materials, they can show visitors the ads that were produced. They can then ask the participants if these had motivated their attendance. All of these methods need to have a staff member present to explain how the prompts relate to answering the question. Before asking these questions, the staff member should introduce themselves and quickly explain the purpose of the interview. They then should explain what type of participant is needed and why.

It is easy to think of asking visitor questions about home location, number of people in the group and how long they stayed. These questions are quick and easy to ask in a survey as visitors leave the event. An interview provides the opportunity to ask detailed questions that will help plan more successful events in the future. A smaller number of existing event visitors can be asked to participate in this longer interview. They can be motivated to participate by offering them a cold drink, a discount to the next event or a small souvenir.

Asking how they heard of the event and what finally motivated them to attend can help the next marketing campaign target visitors more effectively. The popularity of the various activities that were on offer can be gauged by asking the visitor to rank their top three favorites. Another issue of interest to the local business community that can be addressed during an interview is where else visitors spent money. To gather this information, the visitor can be asked where they stayed, where they ate and where they shopped. The visitor should not feel as though they are being interrogated. Instead, simply holding a friendly discussion is all that is needed. While this will not provide exact information on money spent, it can provide evidence that the event is benefitting the community.

Visitor assessment

- Observation: Watching what visitors do at the event.
- Social media: Analyzing postings and reviews.
- Surveys: Asking visitors to complete a questionnaire.
- Interview: Spending more time to analyze problems.

Financial and economic assessment

Tourism events must assess both the number of visitors and the expenditure of these visitors. This expenditure is one of the main objectives of holding a tourism event. Of course, the organization has created and kept a budget to track revenue and expenses. During the planning process for the event the budget was analyzed on a regular basis to ensure that both revenue and expenses were as anticipated. After the event, the actual expenses will be compared to what was budgeted. A negative variance occurs when more was spent than anticipated. This variance between the budgeted amount and actual can result from increased costs, such as a higher-than-anticipated venue lease amount or the need to spend more on marketing materials to increase visitation. Hopefully, increased expenses will be offset by increases in revenue. On the revenue side, an increase is usually because of higher attendance and more products sold to visitors. An increase in expenses with no corresponding increase in revenue is a warning sign that should not be ignored (Woodruff 2019). Corrective action needs to be taken by lowering costs or increasing revenue for the next event.

The budget should have been created with separate revenue lines for each activity for which tickets or products were sold. This will allow for the needed corrective action to be specific to the problem. For example, there may have been an account line to record revenue for ticket sales to the regular event and also to a special VIP event. If the revenue from ticket sales for VIP access was low, it may be decided that the tickets should not be sold again at the next event. However, if VIP tickets exceeded revenue projections it might be decided to increase the size of the VIP event next time.

Family tickets, tickets for the elderly and group tickets should also be separately recorded. These can then be analyzed against the expected revenue. If it is found that tickets for the nighttime event did not sell well, while the expenses for remaining open late were high, then the event may end earlier the next time it is held. Analyzing the revenue lines separately and not just looking at total revenue can result in additional profit for the next event.

It might be tempting to only consider the larger sources of revenue, such as ticket sales. It should be remembered that even when events are financially successful, the amount of profit is usually small. In fact, the event may only be hoping to break even. Because of this, even small sources of revenue can make the difference between success and failure. Additional sources of revenue to track and then analyze would be food and beverage sales. Sponsorship fees from restaurant or lodging establishments that expected to gain sales from the event should be tracked to see if it is worthwhile to pursue this source of funding in the future. Adding booking fees to ticket sales, while not popular with purchasers, may be found to have produced enough revenue to offset the cost of the technology that was paid to handle bookings. Marketing souvenir t-shirts and memorabilia on the event website can also be found to produce the additional revenue that makes the event financially successful. In addition, another revenue stream that should be analyzed is the amount received from selling advertising opportunities where local companies placed their own signage at the event.

Economic impact

Financial impact and economic impact are different measures of success. Financial success is internal to the organization. This will determine if the revenue brought in by tickets, product sales, sponsorships and other sources meet budgeted projections. Of course, it is critical for an event to meet its financial goals if it is going to be held again in the future. Economic benefit is a separate measure of how the community benefits financially from the event being held. Often, tourism and hospitality organizations will state that events provide an economic benefit to the community without providing any proof.

There are three ways to study economic impact. The first is direct impact. This is the money that is directly spent as a result of visitor attendance. This does not include the money that is received by the organization holding the event; it includes where else the visitors spent money while in the community. This would include lodging and restaurant meals. It would also include transportation expenses such as fuel and parking. There would be other ways that visitors might spend money. For example, the visitors could spend money by buying tickets to see other attractions. They could also spend money at local stores for souvenirs of their experiences. In addition, they could shop for necessities, such as picking up food at a market or supplies at a store. All of this is new money coming in to the community that provides an economic benefit.

It is critical to separate out money spent by visitors from money spent by local residents. Within a community, the people who live there only have a certain amount of money they can spend on entertainment. If they spend some of their budget to attend the event, this will certainly increase revenue. However, this means that some other entertainment choices in the community will not have received this revenue. It may be that local residents decide to attend the event rather than spend their money traveling outside the area. In this case, the money spent would be directly attributable to the event as otherwise the money would have left the community (Demski 2019). If the local resident had spent money traveling to another destination, the money would have been lost to the community.

Visitors coming into the community bring in new money. This will be spent directly at the event and at other businesses. This is the economic benefit that must be tracked. An easy way to do so is to ensure that any ticket sales include geographic information on the purchaser. This will provide an idea of the percentage of direct revenue attributable to visitors. Lodging establishments can also be asked to provide information on the geographic information on guests. Guests can also be asked directly if they have traveled to the destination for the event.

Information on the amount of money spent by visitors at other locations can be more difficult to ascertain. Busy restaurant servers cannot be asked to keep track of where diners are from and the amount spent. However, it can be determined if expenditures are higher than they would normally have been if the event had not been held. While there is no way to know exactly how much the local economy has gained, the effort still must be made.

There is another measure of total economic impact that is difficult for a single organization to measure. The new money brought into the community and spent at local establishments increases their revenue. They may in turn increase their expenditures in the community. They may hire and pay additional local residents as staff, who will then have more money to spend. Local businesses may also decide to use their increased revenue received from visitors to improve their facilities. If they hire local companies to do the work, this again increases wealth in the community. A final measure is tax impact. All of this economic spending will result in increased tax revenue for the government.

Community and environmental assessment

While local residents are welcomed at events, they are not the primary target market segment for a tourism event. Local residents do add to attendance numbers and also contribute to the visit experience. Visitors are often attracted to events that attract locals as such events are considered more authentic. While event sponsors and the community will be impressed when a high number of visitors is recorded, the event goals may require a more sophisticated analysis.

One goal for the event may have been to bring in visitors from outside the community. In contrast, the goal might have been to increase the number of local visitors. To provide this analysis there needs to be a means of tracking the home location of visitors. If the event requires paid ticketing, this can be a simple process. The address, or at least the geographic area code, can be collected as part of the purchase process. When the event is free, the collection of such data is more challenging. However, for all tourism events this is essential information.

One source of information is to ask visitors staying at hotels where they are from. This method will not capture local event attendees. To collect this data, it may be necessary to use volunteers to gather this information at the point of entry into the event. This can be done by simply asking people where they are from. At a large event it may not be possible to get this information from everyone, but even a sample of visitors will provide some insight into whether the attendance goals have been achieved.

If part of the event goals was to attract visitors from a specific age or ethnic group, the process of accessing data becomes increasingly difficult. Not only will visitors be unwilling to share this data, they may be offended when asked. The best that can be done in this situation is to use observational research and visually access the audience at the event.

Once these numbers have been gathered, they need to be compared with the goals that were set. It is easy to focus on how much the event was enjoyed and then ignore low attendance. If the numbers were lower than expected, this does not mean that the event was a failure. First, the attendance results must be compared with other goals. For example, the attendance may have been lower than expected but the financial goals may have still been met because of increased spending per visitor. External forces beyond the control of the organization might also have affected attendance. Attendance might have been negatively affected due to an unexpected storm or transportation strike.

If attendance is low the first time an event is held, the organization should not immediately assume that the event was a failure. If visitors were happy with the event, the problem might be solved by improved marketing outreach for the next event. Photos of people enjoying the event, along with testimonials, can be used in marketing to increase attendance.

If visitor numbers were low and survey results show that people were not pleased with the experience, then careful consideration must be given as to whether the event should be held again. This is not a situation where the organizing staff should be made to feel badly. Instead, they should be commended for all the time and work that went into the effort. Then planning should begin for the next event that will be better, based on what has been learned.

Environmental impact

One of the assessments that needs to be conducted is the environmental impact of the event. There are several reasons that event organizers are committed to lessening environment impacts (O'Mahoney 2017). The first would be their own personal values. They might also be influenced by consumer demand because of environmental awareness. Lastly, doing so provides a competitive advantage. The mission and values statement, along with promotional material, may have stated that the organization was committed to minimizing the environmental impact of the event. Only the assessment will prove that the commitment resulted in real positive action and a lessening of effects. Three areas to address are transportation, waste management and product sourcing.

The organization cannot control how people travel to the event. If people drive, it will cause an increase in traffic and the need for additional parking space. The event planning process should have addressed the need to lessen traffic by providing transportation alternatives. One way to reduce traffic is to provide information on local cycling routes that can be used, along with providing bike racks. The number of bikes that have used these rakes can then be counted. Local bus routes can be provided, along with train routes. Checking with these transportation providers can provide information on any increase of passengers on the routes to the event.

The organization should have a plan for addressing waste management. This is needed to meet environmental goals. Also, a litter-filled venue will detract from the visitor experience. Of course, as much as possible recyclable material should be used. Before the event, the organizers should ensure that there are sufficient trash and recycling receptacles. A measure of success would if a high percentage of all trash collected is in the recycling bins.

Lastly, the sourcing of any physical products that are sold along with food and beverage has an environmental effect. The longer the distance that any physical goods such as tote bags, t-shirts and souvenirs have to travel, the less sustainable they are. There will be price constraint as goods produced closer to the event site may be more costly. This increased cost may increase product prices, but this information should be provided to the visitor who may then be willing to pay. Visitors are also interested in consuming local food and beverage for several reasons, one of which is they have less of an environmental impact. After the event, the percentage of all goods, food and beverages that were sourced locally should be calculated.

Sponsorship evaluation

Finally, sponsor satisfaction should also be evaluated. The funding from sponsors can be critical in meeting the revenue goals and balancing the budget for the event. If sponsors are again going to provide funding, they need to feel that they have received value for their money. Personal visits or phone calls to event sponsors should be scheduled for as soon after the event as possible. Sponsors should be asked their overall opinion of the event. They should then be asked if the event met their expectations. This might be the number of people with which they were able to personally interact. Rather than personal contact, sponsors' goals might have been to build awareness so that sales would be made at a later date. If so, the organizers should contact the sponsors in a few months to see if sales increased.

The organizers should welcome any feedback from the sponsors that can be used to improve the event in the future. It might be decided that the event was not a good match for the sponsoring company. In this case, the organizers would thank them for their past support. The organization should remain in contact as the company personnel and strategy can change in the future.

Discussion questions

1. Why is it important to perform the needed administrative tasks once the event has concluded?
2. What physical tasks need to be done when the event has ended?
3. Why might the decision be made not to hold the event again?
4. How can observation of visitors at the event help improve the next event?
5. What is the reason for surveying past event visitors?
6. In what type of situations is interviewing guests after the event helpful?
7. Although difficult to do, why is an assessment of the economic benefits to the community critical?
8. What questions could be asked of sponsors after the event has concluded?

Getting the views of everyone when assessing success

At the end of the event, organizers will ask each other, "How do you think it went?" While such feedback is valid, it is common to also get feedback from visitors. However, there are even more people that should be asked their opinions. The information received can then be combined with quantitative data such as attendance and revenue figures. Here are some groups that should be surveyed and topics that should be explored.

- Visitors: Why did they choose to attend the event? This information will help to assess promotional effectiveness. What benefits did they receive from attending? If the event had many components be sure to ask about each separately.
- Volunteers: How did they feel they were treated by organizers? Were they confused by what was required? Their opinions can make the next event be even better organized as they will have the best knowledge.
- Sponsors/partners: Did the type of visitors at the event meet their expectations? Are they interested in sponsoring or partnering again? The needs of sponsors and partners are very different from those of visitors. Without asking, it is impossible to know if their expectations were met or if the event was a waste of their resources.
- Entertainers/speakers: Were their equipment needs met? What could be done to enhance their experience at the next event? While planning is critical, it is only when the event actually happens that problem areas may be discovered (Waida 2018).

Task: What survey questions should be included in your event assessment survey?

Writing a post-event report

As soon as possible after the event a report should be written summarizing both successes and problems. This report can provide ideas for improving the next event. It can also be provided to partner organizations to encourage their future participation. A third reason for writing the report is that it can be used as a template for planning the next event. It should include the following components.

- Introduction: This portion should be short and focus on whether the event objectives were met. Some people only read this section as they are not interested in the details.
- Attendance: Here will be the place to include overall attendance numbers. If possible, they should also be broken down by visitor segment. If a multi-day event, they should also be by date.
- Finances: This section will start with a statement on whether the financial goals were met. It will also include a variance report describing areas of savings and ones of overspending.
- Venue/location: Any problems with the venue or location should be noted. This will help with the decision as to whether to make a change for the next event.
- Activities: Using survey data, it should be noted which events were popular with visitors and which did not draw a crowd. There is no reason to repeat an activity and instead it can be replaced with something new.
- Marketing: Hopefully visitors will be asked how they learned about the event. In addition, the metrics from social media sites will help inform the decision of where and how to promote the next event (Tomakh 2019).

Task: Create a template that can be used for a post-event report.

Event plan: Use the information from this chapter to complete the first section of the event plan outline at the end of the book.

References

Byvalkevych, Irene. 2019. "Questions for a Successful Event Debrief." *Gevme*. September 30, 2019. https://www.gevme.com/blog/questions-for-a-successful-event-debrief/ Accessed November 14, 2020.

Demski, Joe. 2019. "What Value Do Community Events Provide?" *Implan Blog*. July 26, 2019. https://blog.implan.com/community-event-impact. Accessed November 12, 2020.

McDonald, Scott. 2018. "The Voice of the Customer Still Matters." *Forbes*. May 29, 2018. https://www.forbes.com/sites/scottmcdonald1/2018/05/29/the-voice-of-customer-still-matters/?sh=41fab52d7481. Accessed August 14, 2020.

O'Mahoney, Sinead. 2017. "The Environmental Impact of Events." *Cuckoo*. October 6, 2017. https://www.cuckoo.ie/blog/event-related/environmental-impacts-events.html. Accessed September 30, 2020.

Tomakh, Anna. 2019. "How to Write a Post Event Report to Get Actionable Insights." *GEVME*. June 12, 2019. https://www.gevme.com/blog/how-to-write-a-post-event-report-to-get-actionable-insights/. Accessed October 23, 2020.

Waida, Maria. 2018. "20 Questions to Ask Your Attendees, Sponsors & Stakeholders." *The Bizzabo Blog*. November 15, 2018. https://blog.bizzabo.com/event-survey-questions. Accessed December 12, 2020.

Wong, Michelle. 2019. "Evaluating Event Success: What to Measure and When." *Eventmobi*. April 3, 2019. https://www.eventmobi.com/blog/evaluating-event-success-what-to-measure-and-when/. Accessed December 22, 2020.

Woodruff, Jim. 2019. "What is Variance Analysis?" *Small Business Chronicle*. January 25, 2019. https://smallbusiness.chron.com/budget-variance-analysis-60250.html. Accessed August 7, 2019.

Event plan outline

Each number in the list refers to a chapter. Try to start on each section once the chapter is read. You will need to continually go back and revise as your ideas develop. By the end of reading the book you will be able to develop a complete event plan.

1. Event purpose: Why are you having an event?
   a. Describe the purpose of your event.
   b. List the aspects of the community that will need to be improved.
2. Event type: What type of event will you have?
   a. Describe the core event and its benefits.
   b. List the other community features and services to be included.
3. Goals and objectives: What are your objectives and tasks from the SWOT?
   a. List the strengths and weaknesses of your proposed event.
   b. List the external opportunities and threats you face.
   c. Describe at least three objectives and the tasks that will be needed for each.
4. Targeted visitor segment Who is your targeted visitor segment?
   a. State whether you will have a concentrated or multi-segmented strategy.
   b. Describe the demographic, geographic and psychographic traits of your visitors.
5. Research plan: What research to you need to conduct?
   a. Write your research question.
   b. Describe the type of research and what will be asked.
6. Pricing/budget: What is your budget for the event and how much will you charge?
   a. Describe your pricing strategy.
   b. List your sources of revenue and expenses.
7. Venue/activities: Where will your event be held and what will there be to do?
   a. Describe the venue for your event.
   b. List the activities that will be available.
   c. List the food and beverage options.
8. Issues/agenda: What is the agenda for the day(s)?
   a. Describe how you will handle issues of concern to your visitors.
   b. Develop a planning calendar starting six months before the event.
   c. List an agenda for the day with responsibilities and staffing.
9. Marketing message: What is your marketing message?
   a. List the features, benefits and values of your event.
   b. Describe the brand image and words that will be used in promotion.

10. Traditional media How will you use traditional media?
    a. Describe ideas for using advertising, sales incentives and personal selling.
    b. Describe how public relations can be used to build awareness.
11. Social media: What social media will you use?
    a. List the social media sites that will be used.
    b. Create a content marketing calendar.
12. Event assessment: How will you assess the success of the event?
    a. List the administrative and physical tasks needed at the end of the event.
    b. Describe how the event success will be analyzed.

Index

Printed in the United States
by Baker & Taylor Publisher Services